The Development of Women's Soccer

While women's soccer has risen in popularity around the world, research reveals persistent gender discrimination and marginalization of girls and women in the sport. Applying policy feedback theory and econometric analysis, this volume explores the lasting impact of different regimes of gender discrimination on the development of women's soccer in Germany.

Taking reunified Germany as an ideal case for examining the long-term impact of policy legacies, the book explores how the different systems of gender discrimination in divided Germany have influenced the participation and popularity of women's soccer. It analyzes the development of grass-roots girls' and women's soccer in different regions, and examines the development of the semi-professional Frauen-Bundesliga and the popularity of the national women's soccer team, which serves as the most important outlet for women's soccer in Germany. Drawing on these analyses, the book assesses the impact of policy legacies, identifies key challenges for the future of women's soccer and offers some practical directions for future development. The evidence presented in this book suggests that the sport has experienced substantial long-term growth but is now in a period of stagnation. The book argues that discrimination against girls' and women's soccer has long-lasting effects and that the policy priorities adopted by soccer's governing bodies, local clubs, as well as television operators, have huge significance for the longer-term development of the game.

This is fascinating reading for students and researchers of sport sociology, women's sport, sports economics, sport development, sport management, and gender studies as well as decision makers within the soccer sector. It is also a valuable resource for scholars, policymakers, sport officials, and women's soccer activists.

Henk Erik Meier is Professor of Social Sciences of Sport at the Institute for Sport and Exercise Sciences at the University of Münster, Germany.

Critical Research in Football

Series Editors: Pete Millward, *Liverpool John Moores University, UK*
Jamie Cleland, *University of South Australia*
Dan Parnell, *University of Liverpool, UK*
Stacey Pope, *Durham University, UK*
Paul Widdop, *Manchester Metropolitan University, UK*

The *Critical Research in Football* book series was launched in 2017 to showcase the inter- and multi-disciplinary breadth of debate relating to 'football'. The series defines 'football' as broader than association football, with research on rugby, Gaelic, and gridiron codes also featured. Including monographs, edited collections, short books, and textbooks, books in the series are written and/or edited by leading experts in the field whilst consciously also affording space to emerging voices in the area, and are designed to appeal to students, postgraduate students, and scholars who are interested in the range of disciplines in which critical research in football connects. The series is published in association with the *Football Collective*, www.footballcollective.org.uk.

Available in this series:

Football in Fiction
A History
Lee McGowan

Football as Medicine
Prescribing Football for Global Health Promotion
Edited by Peter Krustrup and Daniel Parnell

Politics, Ideology and Football Fandom
The Transformation of Modern Poland
Radosław Kossakowski, Przemysław Nosal and Wojciech Woźniak

The Development of Women's Soccer
Legacies, Participation, and Popularity in Germany
Henk Erik Meier

www.routledge.com/sport/series/CFSFC

The Development of Women's Soccer
Legacies, Participation, and Popularity in Germany

Henk Erik Meier

LONDON AND NEW YORK

First published 2020
by Routledge
2 Park Square, Milton Park, Abingdon, Oxon OX14 4RN

and by Routledge
605 Third Avenue, New York, NY 10017

First issued in paperback 2021

Routledge is an imprint of the Taylor & Francis Group, an informa business

Copyright © 2020 Henk Erik Meier

The right of Henk Erik Meier to be identified as authors of this work
has been asserted by him in accordance with sections 77 and 78 of the
Copyright, Designs and Patents Act 1988.

All rights reserved. No part of this book may be reprinted or reproduced
or utilised in any form or by any electronic, mechanical, or other means,
now known or hereafter invented, including photocopying and recording,
or in any information storage or retrieval system, without permission in
writing from the publishers.

Trademark notice: Product or corporate names may be trademarks or
registered trademarks, and are used only for identification and explanation
without intent to infringe.

Publisher's Note
The publisher has gone to great lengths to ensure the quality of this reprint
but points out that some imperfections in the original copies may be
apparent.

British Library Cataloguing-in-Publication Data
A catalogue record for this book is available from the British Library

Library of Congress Cataloging-in-Publication Data
Names: Meier, Henk Erik, author. | Routledge (Firm)
Title: The development of women's soccer : legacies, participation
and popularity in Germany / Henk Erik Meier.
Description: First Edition. | New York : Routledge, 2020. |
Includes bibliographical references and index. |
Identifiers: LCCN 2019056629 (print) | LCCN 2019056630 (ebook) |
ISBN 9780367357351 (Hardback) | ISBN 9780429341403 (eBook)
Subjects: LCSH: Soccer for women–Germany–History. |
Soccer for women–Social aspects. | Feminism and sports. | Soccer–History. |
Soccer–Social aspects. | Soccer players–United States. |
Soccer players–Germany. | Feminism–Germany. | Language and culture.
Classification: LCC GV944.5 .M43 2020 (print) |
LCC GV944.5 (ebook) | DDC 796.334082–dc23
LC record available at https://lccn.loc.gov/2019056629
LC ebook record available at https://lccn.loc.gov/2019056630

ISBN 13: 978-1-03-223840-1 (pbk)
ISBN 13: 978-0-367-35735-1 (hbk)

Typeset in Times New Roman
by Newgen Publishing UK

Contents

	List of figures	*vi*
	List of tables	*vii*
	Preface	*ix*
1	Germany as a natural experiment for the future of women's soccer	1
2	The development of girls' and women's grass-roots soccer	20
3	Stadium attendance in women's league soccer	47
4	The popularity of the women's national soccer team	71
5	How feminine will the future of soccer be?	95
	Appendix	*103*
	References	*130*
	Index	*149*

Figures

1.1	FIFA rankings of women's national soccer teams from 2010 to 2015	2
2.1	German state associations participating in the study	29
2.2	Number of women's and girls' teams in 17 German state associations	32
2.3	Spatial distribution of girl's and women's soccer across Germany	33
2.4	Team survival in German girls' and women's soccer	35
3.1	Competitive balance in the Frauen-Bundesliga	49
3.2	Team survival in the Frauen-Bundesliga	49
3.3	Stadium quality in the Frauen-Bundesliga	58
3.4	Average attendance for matches of the Frauen-Bundesliga	60
4.1	TV ratings for matches of the women's national soccer team from 1995 to 2017	79
4.2	TV ratings for matches of the women's national soccer team from 1995 to 2017	80
4.3	TV ratings for matches of the women's national soccer team from 1995 to 2017	88
4.4	TV ratings for matches of the women's national soccer team from 2003 to 2017	89
A.1	Histogram of TV ratings for matches of the women's national soccer team	126

Tables

1.1	Women's national soccer team performances from 2010 to 2015	5
2.1	The state of girls' and women's soccer in state associations	34
2.2	Analyzing girls' and women's soccer teams per municipality	36
2.3	Analyzing team survival from seasons 2005/2006 to 2015/2016	40
2.4	Girls' and women's soccer team survival from seasons 2011/2012 to 2015/2016	42
3.1	Changes in team affiliations in the Frauen-Bundesliga	56
3.2	Attendance for Frauen-Bundesliga matches	61
3.3	Semi-elasticities and elasticities for demand for Frauen-Bundesliga matches	66
4.1	MANOVA of TV ratings for matches of the women's national soccer team	81
4.2	TV ratings for matches of the women's national soccer team from 1995 to 2017	81
4.3	TV ratings for matches of the women's national soccer team from 2003 to 2017	85
A.1	Dataset on women's national soccer team performances from 2010 to 2015	104
A.2	The count dataset—girls' and women's soccer teams per municipality	108
A.3	Coding of the unified league indicator	109
A.4	The survival dataset—girls' and women's soccer team dissolution	110
A.5	Stadium attendance in the Frauen-Bundesliga: Dependent and independent variables	116

viii   *List of tables*

A.6	Popularity of the women's national soccer team: Dependent and independent variables	123
A.7	Determining correlation structure—women between 3 and 50 years	127
A.8	Determining model—women between 3 and 50 years	127
A.9	Determining correlation structure—women older than 50 years	128
A.10	Determining model—women older than 50 years	128
A.11	Determining correlation structure—men between 3 and 50 years	128
A.12	Determining model—men between 3 and 50 years	128
A.13	Determining correlation structure—men older than 50 years	129
A.14	Determining model—men older than 50 years	129

Preface

I have been inspired to conduct research on women's soccer by my own love for soccer and the blatant lack of statistical works on women's sport. When I started doing research on women's soccer, there existed an impressive stock of brilliant historical and ethnographic scholarship but not much macro-sociological or economic research. By now, scholars have increasingly dedicated their efforts to women's sport and have presented innovative and highly instructive studies. Although people who are more brilliant than me have contributed better research to the academic debate, I still feel encouraged to present what might be called a statistical case study on the development and popularity of women's soccer in Germany. Germany is, by nature one might say, a powerhouse of women's soccer. Besides a strong national soccer tradition, Germany is one of the wealthiest and most gender-equal countries in the world. However, as this book tries to illustrate, such favorable macro-social conditions do not guarantee that 'the future of soccer will be feminine', as the now infamous President of the world soccer association Fédération Internationale de Football Association (FIFA) Joseph ('Sepp') Blatter once claimed (Degele, 2012). Over recent years, the German women's national soccer team has delivered a streak of rather disappointing performances, nurturing the impression that Germany has lost its leading position in women's soccer. The 2019 FIFA Women's World Cup—during which the German team was beaten in the quarter-final by Sweden—has provoked a debate about the future of women's soccer in Germany. Active soccer participation by girls and women, as well as public attention to the sport, are stagnating. Hence, Germany defies the optimistic prediction that the future of soccer will be automatically more female. In addition, Germany is characterized by a persistent cultural divide in sporting traditions between West and East Germany illustrating the lasting impact of communist sport policy legacies. Hence, the book illustrates that the development of girls' and

x *Preface*

women's soccer is not a linear process. Rather, policymakers enjoy substantial discretion and their choices matter.

I am heavily indebted to a number of colleagues from the Institute of Sport and Exercise Sciences at the University of Münster without whose support I would not have been able to write this book. I benefitted heavily from Michael Krüger's outstanding expertise in German and international sport history. Michael helped me to understand the wider issues and larger contexts of West German sport history and has been a profound teacher over the years. Moreover, it proved very advantageous for me that Michael had been awarded a project on soccer history in East Germany. The discussions with Kai Reinhart and Justus Kalthoff about the oral history of East German soccer were very helpful. The collaboration with Bernd Strauß on several papers on soccer fans proved to be most inspiring for this book. Bernd motivated me to develop my ideas about secular changes in sport consumption and to take on the challenges of more advanced statistical modeling. Mara Konjer has been an inspiring and reliable collaborator and part of my team over the years.

In addition, a number of collaborators contributed to the construction of the datasets analyzed here. My former student assistant Marcel Leinwather helped with the construction of the datasets on stadium attendance and television (TV) ratings. Marcel has been extremely capable when it came to gathering data. Among others, he assumed the difficult task of tracing the development of stadium facilities in women's first-tier league soccer. Cosima von Uechtritz provided helpful support when these original datasets had to be updated and extended for this book. Till Ommo Utesch and Stefan Stroth were an invaluable help when it came to conducting the dataset on grass-roots girls' and women's soccer. It was a great comfort to be able to share the frustrations that arose from working with German official statistics. I am also very grateful that Malte Jetzke provided a final makeover to the diagrams presented in the book. Last but not least, I would like to thank my secretary Nerojini Raissi for her diligent and patient support over the years.

I would like to dedicate this book to my youngest daughter Ruth Emilia Bäck who is now playing soccer at Lunds BOIS, the oldest soccer club in Lund, Sweden:

> Kära Emilia, jag gillade verkligen att träna med dig i sommar. Jag hoppas att du fortsätter spela fotboll! Din pappa.

Münster, September 2019

1 Germany as a natural experiment for the future of women's soccer

Introduction

In what might be remembered as one of his more memorable moments, Sepp Blatter, the former president of the world soccer federation (Fédération Internationale de Football Association—FIFA) declared after the women's soccer World Championship in 1995, that 'the future of soccer is feminine' (see also FIFA, 2011). This often-cited quote should not be misinterpreted as signaling that FIFA has ceased to be an institution of male hegemony (Fink, 2008; Williams, 2014). Hence, the slightly derogative attitude among FIFA officials toward women's soccer became evident when Blatter reasoned that female soccer was to be best marketed by emphasizing the players' attractiveness or feminine qualities (Fink, 2015). Moreover, given FIFA's character as a transnational revenue-maximizing corporation, the new interest in women's soccer might simply represent the search for new customers in an increasingly saturated sports entertainment market. Nevertheless, given a long history of some soccer governing bodies' toward women playing soccer, Blatter's statement in favor of women's soccer seems remarkable. Therefore, the question of how much truth lies in the 'future of soccer is feminine' claim defines the *leitmotif* of this book.

Seen from a macro-sociological perspective, the idea that the future of soccer will be (more) female seems encouraged, insofar as the development of women's soccer appears to be linked to social progress, in particular to increased gender equality. Figure 1.1 relates the annual FIFA rankings of women's national soccer teams in the period between 2010 and 2015 to the national Gender Inequality Value (GIV) as conducted by the United Nations Educational, Scientific, and Cultural Organization (UNESCO). The GIV accounts for gender inequalities in the dimensions of reproductive health, empowerment, and labor market and would assume zero in the case of perfect gender equality

2 Germany as a natural experiment

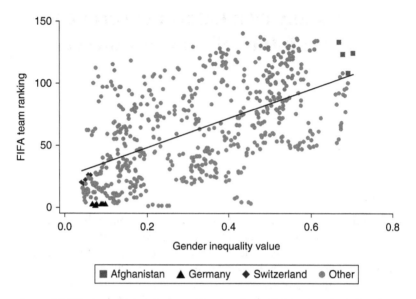

Figure 1.1 FIFA rankings of women's national soccer teams from 2010 to 2015

Note: 463 observations for the period 2010 to 2015. FIFA rankings provided by FIFA's official website. Gender inequality index provided by the United Nations Educational, Scientific, and Cultural Organization (UNESCO).

and one in the case of total gender inequality (for more detail, see UNESCO, 2011). The diagram shows a moderate linear relationship between gender inequality and women's soccer team performances ($r = 0.581$; $p < 0.001$). Hence, more gender-equal societies tend to have better performing women's soccer teams. The most gender unequal country included in Figure 1.1 is Afghanistan with a GIV of 0.701 in 2012. Afghanistan achieved its best FIFA ranking (108th) in 2013. The most gender-equal country is Switzerland with a GVI of 0.040 in 2015. The Swiss women's soccer team achieved its best FIFA ranking (19th) in 2014. According to the GIV, Germany represents one of the most gender-equal societies—its lowest GIV equaled 0.066 in 2015—and has occupied the second or first rank among all women's teams in the period between 2010 and 2015. In addition, it is instructive to notice that countries that field no national team in a regular FIFA competition at all, are characterized by significantly higher levels of gender inequality as a simple analysis of variance (ANOVA) reveals ($F_{1,311} = 204.26$; $p < 0.001$; $N = 1{,}312$).

Germany as a natural experiment 3

The insight that gender inequality is decisive for success in women's sport is hardly new. As gender discrimination is often related to the suppression of female participation in sport, gender equality has proven to be an important factor for achieving success in women's sport. In a groundbreaking paper, Klein (2004) demonstrated that female labor force participation related to better female performances in the Summer Olympics and the Women's World Cup, even when he controlled for income per capita and population size. The latter variables have been proven to be the most valid predictors of national athletic performances. According to the parsimonious economic model for explaining the production of athletic success, population size defines the national pool of athletic talents, while national wealth provides the economic means to develop these very talents. In addition, membership in the communist bloc has served as a proxy either for organizational capacities or for policy priorities in favor of elite sports policies (Bernard & Busse, 2004).

Based on a larger sample and a higher number of control variables, Leeds and Leeds (2012) confirmed that higher female labor force participation related to improved female performances at the Summer Olympics. Moreover, they found that lower fertility rates and a longer tradition of women suffrage correlated with better female performances. Noland and Stahler (2016) used similar measures in their more recent analyses of female performances at the Summer Olympics and found that the socio-economic status of women was a decisive predictor. In contrast, Lowen et al. (2016) used the gender inequality value (GIV), which is also employed here, as predictor for success in the Summer Olympics. They could again confirm that greater gender equality is consistently and significantly associated with improvements in two measures of Olympic success, athlete participation and medal counts, even when other important predictors were taken into account. Moreover, they even found that higher gender inequality reduces the number of medals won by both men and women. The fact that Islamic religion does not support female sport participation might also explain why Islamic religion has been found to be a negative predictor of sporting success in the Olympics (Sfeir, 1985; Tcha & Pershin, 2003; Trivedi & Zimmer, 2014; Noland & Stahler, 2016).

With regard to women's soccer, the small number of available studies has confirmed Klein's (2004) basic insight that gender equality relates to better performances of women's national soccer teams.[1] Analyzing the scores awarded to national women's soccer teams by the FIFA ranking system, Hoffmann et al. (2006) found that the ratio of average women's earnings to men's earning had a significant impact on team performances. Hence, the lower the gender pay gap, the better national

4 *Germany as a natural experiment*

team performances. In the context of this book, it is further relevant that Hoffmann and colleagues (2006) detected a political system effect according to which countries, which previously or presently had a communist or socialist system, performed better in women's soccer. In an ambitious article, which compared determinants of men's and women's team performances as measured by FIFA scores, Congdon-Hohman and Matheson (2013) used the ratio of female to male secondary enrollment rates as an indicator for gender equality. They found that the influence of economic and demographic factors is similar for men's and women's team performances. In constrast, Muslim religious affiliation reduced women's success but not men's, while communist political systems tended to improve women's performances but to reduce men's. The gender equality indicator used seemed to exert a positive impact on women's soccer performance but not on men's. Since other gender equality indicators were related to improved women's and men's performances, Congdon-Hohman and Matheson (2013) concluded that these indicators reflect overall levels of development.

Cho (2013) also used FIFA scores to examine the question whether soccer traditions or women's empowerment were a driving force for national success in female soccer. Again female labor force participation served as a proxy for gender equality. The results contradicted the assumption of a decisive impact on female performance in soccer from the male soccer legacy. Cho (2013: 10) concluded that the findings

> indicate that women's empowerment promotes the success of female soccer, particularly in countries with strong soccer tradition. My study suggests that female soccer is not a byproduct of male soccer, rather it has developed its own path alongside with overall women's advancement.

Jacobs (2014) has presented an ambitious study evaluating the effect of FIFA programs for promoting women's soccer. Again, FIFA scores served as the dependent variable. Jacobs (2014) detected a significant impact of the institutional factor on women's team performances. Dedicated governance staff and training proved to be key correlates of successful women's soccer nations in the short term, while dedicated governance staff and investments in youth developments were strong predictors in the long term. At the macro level, income per capita, female population, and female labor force participation were consistently and positively associated with women's team success.

The simple multivariate analyses conducted for this chapter strongly support the fundamental insight that macro-social gender equality is

Germany as a natural experiment 5

a positive correlate of national athletic success in women's soccer. In contrast to previous accounts, annual FIFA rankings—not scores—served as the dependent variable in several random-effects ordered logistic regressions. Naturally, these simple models cannot compete with the more sophisticated analyses just discussed. However, they are instructive, insofar as they suggest that gender equality is more decisive for national team performances than national income per capita. Yet, the data conducted support the claim made by Congdon-Hohman and Matheson (2013) that gender equality measures reflect overall levels of development. Hence, in the dataset analyzed here, GDP per capita was moderately correlated with lower gender inequality as measured by the GIV ($r = -0.614$; $p < 0.001$; Table 1.1).

So far, it can be concluded that macro-social gender equality is related to the performance of women's national soccer teams. More gender-equal countries tend to perform better. Accordingly, if it could be assumed that societies progress toward more gender equality, Blatter would have been right with his prediction that the future of soccer would indeed be (more) female. Unfortunately, UNESCO's data indicate only a marginal decrease of gender inequality over the period from 2010 to 2015.

For the potential contribution of a case study on women's soccer in Germany to the general debate about the sports' prospect, it is relevant that previous research has consistently found that there exists a significant relationship between the development of women's soccer on the one

Table 1.1 Women's national soccer team performances from 2010 to 2015

Independent variables	Model 1	Model 2	Model 3
Gender inequality value[a]	21.016***		22.042***
	(3.815)		(4.311)
GDP per capita in 1,000 USD[b]		–0.066	0.025
		(0.036)	(0.040)
Country share of world population[b]	–1.462**	–1.527**	–1.433**
	(0.494)	(0.540)	(0.496)
N	613	679	604
Number of groups	129	140	128
Observations per group	4.8	4.8	4.7

Notes: *** $p < 0.001$; ** $p < 0.01$; * $p < 0.05$. Dependent variable is the FIFA rank of the women's national soccer team. Method is panel ordinal logistic regression with random effects using STATA's xtologit command. FIFA rankings as provided by FIFA's official website. a. Gender inequality index as provided by the United Nations Educational, Scientific, and Cultural Organization (UNESCO). b. Data on GDP per capita and population were retrieved from the Human Development Report's website (UNDP, 2018).

6 *Germany as a natural experiment*

hand and population size and GDP per capita on the other. Accordingly, the future of women's soccer can be realistically assessed by examining countries characterized by (comparably) low gender inequality and high levels of socio-economic development. Seen from this perspective, Germany represents an ideal case for studying the prospects of women's soccer. Germany is one of the wealthiest countries in the world and one with the lowest degrees of gender inequality. Moreover, Germany has constantly occupied first or second place in FIFA's rankings of women's national teams since these rankings were introduced in 2003. Germany's women's national soccer team has won the Olympic soccer tournament, the FIFA Women's World Cup twice, and the Women's EURO of the Union of European Football Associations (UEFA) eight times. Thus, the conditions for women's soccer seem to be rather favorable in Germany. Accordingly, research presented here will analyze German data on the state and development of women's soccer in order to determine how female the future of soccer might actually be.

An additional rationale for examining Germany is that the country represents a natural experiment or, more precisely, an ideal comparative case study for studying the impact of different institutional legacies on the development of women's soccer. After 40 years of division, the reunification of Germany in 1990 placed two very different societies under the West German regime. The transfer of West German institutions has since then raised the question of how East German attitudes and behaviors would adapt (Konietzka & Kreyenfeld, 2002; Lee et al., 2007; Bauernschuster & Rainer, 2011; Hanel & Riphan, 2011). Research in different societal domains has provided evidence for convergence as well as persistent divergence of attitudes and behaviors. Hence, East Germans favor a more expansive role of the state, they are also more critical concerning the functioning of the democratic process and more hostile to immigration (Gabriel, 2007; Dalton & Weldon, 2010; Campbell, 2015).

With regard to sports, it is relevant that the sport-centered identity politics of the communist German Democratic Republic (GDR— henceforth: East Germany) seem to have left persistent legacies. Hence, pride in athletic achievements is still more important for East Germans (Meier & Mutz 2016). However, East Germany was mostly successful in Olympic sports but could never compete with the national team of the Federal Republic of Germany (FRG—henceforth: West Germany). These differences in athletic success continue to show in the substantially lower popularity of the men's national soccer team in East Germany (Meier, Reinhart et al., 2016). In order to examine the impact of institutional legacies on the development of women's soccer, it is most relevant

Germany as a natural experiment 7

that the two Germanys had adopted quite different and slightly contradictory policies regarding gender relations and women's soccer. These divergent policies will be discussed in the following sections.

German gender policies before and after reunification

After World War II, the two Germanys implemented highly different gender regimes. Notwithstanding a substantial modernization of gender roles in reunified Germany, the legacies of these contrasting gender regimes have materialized in persistent differences in gender-role attitudes between West and East Germans.

After the Nazi's 'total war' effort had required higher female labor force participation, social conservatism prevailed in West Germany and aimed at restoring traditional gender roles. Women were relegated to unpaid homemaking and men to breadwinning (Rosenfeld et al., 2004: 104). Through a combination of tax, social insurance, and family policies, West Germany implemented a highly unequal gender regime that discouraged in particular mothers from labor force participation (Konietzka & Kreyenfeld, 2002). Despite the social upheaval since the 1960s, social conservatism continued to dominate gender policies until 1998 when a red–green coalition replaced the conservative-liberal government of Helmut Kohl. Since then, Germany has adopted a number of laws aiming to facilitate and promote the labor force participation of women. The erosion of the traditional male breadwinner model was further catalyzed by a deregulation of labor market laws and a reform of welfare benefits. Moreover, childcare provision has been heavily expanded (Busse & Gathmann, 2018). As a result, female part-time work turned into an 'ever more important source of supplementary income to that of the male earner' (Trappe et al., 2015: 233).

In East Germany, full emancipation of women was an official rhetoric goal of socialist ideology (Braun et al., 1994). Moreover, the East German communists adopted a policy of state-decreed professional emancipation mainly due to the permanent shortage of labor (Rosenfeld et al., 2004). Thus, mothers were encouraged to take on high levels of employment and long weekly hours through the provision of childcare facilities, which resulted in the highest female employment rate in the world (Lee et al., 2007). Therefore, in East Germany occupational segregation and the gender pay gap substantially decreased (Braun et al., 1994). Moreover, professional careers of men and women converged (Trappe & Rosenfeld, 2000). Some East German women even acquired the role of family providers (Konietzka & Kreyenfeld, 2002). However, it is important to note that East German gender policies were far from

8 *Germany as a natural experiment*

consistent (Budde, 2000). The communist regime addressed women as workers *and* mothers, and tried to increase birth rates (Trappe et al., 2015). Moreover, state-decreed professional emancipation did not include changes to male gender roles with regard to family work and household chores (Braun et al., 1994; Lee et al., 2007).

Although East Germany represented not a completely gender-equal society, its gender regime left lasting legacies. The fact is all the more remarkable as economic conditions are rather unfavorable in East Germany and several policy reforms with regard to labor market regulations, parental leave, and childcare provision should promote some convergence between West and East Germany (Zoch & Schober, 2018). Although policies in reunified Germany were destined to result in a 'reversion towards a less gender-equal division of labour in the East' (Trappe et al., 2015: 233), citizens of former communist regions hold more egalitarian gender role attitudes and support the labor force participation of mothers (Rosenfeld et al., 2004; Geisler & Kreyenfeld, 2005; Bauernschuster & Rainer, 2011; Trappe et al., 2015; Barth & Trübner, 2018). Women in East Germany have kept their attachment to the labor force even under unfavorable conditions (Konietzka & Kreyenfeld, 2002; Lee et al., 2007; Hanel & Riphan, 2011). Nevertheless, employment patterns among younger cohorts have slightly converged. Thus, labor force participation of West German women gradually increased over time, while East German women, after the economic transformation, partly adjusted to the West German pattern after unification, resulting in an increase in part-time employment and non-employment (Gangl & Ziefle, 2015; Trappe et al., 2015). However, East Germans are still much more likely to show 'extreme' non-traditional gender-role attitudes (Walter, 2018); only less-educated East Germans seem to have adopted more traditional role models (Zoch & Schober, 2018). Although institutional incompatibilities appear to have reduced the spread of the dual-breadwinner model in East Germany (Dieckhoff et al., 2016), it is still substantially more popular than in West Germany (Müller et al., 2018). There is also evidence of a more egalitarian distribution of unpaid work in East Germany (Rosenfeld et al., 2004). Moreover, gender pay gap analyses found not only that the gender pay gap is lower in East Germany and that there is no trend toward convergence (Minkus & Busch-Heizmann, 2018) but also that in many East German districts women earn even more than men (Fuchs et al., 2019). So-called motherhood earning penalties are also lower in East Germany (Budig et al., 2016). However, it might be noticed that East German legacies do not seem to have reduced the 'glass ceiling effect' (Huffman et al., 2017).

Germany as a natural experiment 9

Yet, it is important to take into account that West German legacies clearly dominate in reunified Germany. Accordingly, Germany still represents predominantly the 'male breadwinner' model in terms of childcare services and the division of family labor (Ciccia & Bleijenberg, 2014). Even though West German men's attitudes have substantially changed during the last decades, men's role as primary breadwinner has only been partly challenged (Trappe et al., 2015) and family labor has remained unequally distributed (Pollmann-Schult & Reynolds, 2017). Traditional gender ideology continues to be present even in self-declared equal responsibility partnerships (Haase et al., 2016). Interestingly, the provision of public childcare has not encouraged more female labor market participation (Busse & Gathmann, 2018). Comparative evidence from the Member States of the European Union suggests further that in Germany, labor taxation laws in combination with lack of childcare facilities work to exclude women—more precisely, mothers—from the labor market entirely or to trap them in low-wage or part-time jobs (European Commission, 2017). Moreover, Germany is characterized by one of the highest gender pay-gaps in the European Union (Eurostat, 2018). These findings seem to contradict the depiction of Germany as one of the most gender-equal countries in the world, based on UNESCO's GIV data. However, it is important to take into account that the Member States of the European Union represent a sample of countries with high levels of gender equality by international comparison.

Given the correlation between gender equality and the development of women's soccer, East Germany, due to its more equal gender policies, should have outperformed West Germany in women's soccer even more, as previous macro-social studies suggested a positive impact of the communist past on women's national team performances (Hoffmann et al., 2006; Congdon-Hohman & Matheson, 2013). However, the more gender-equal policies in East Germany did not translate into support for women's soccer. Thus, the German case is interesting because, although both Germanys discriminated against women's soccer for different reasons, women's soccer developed much better in the socially conservative West than in the more gender-equal East.

The development of women's soccer in Germany

Soccer illustrates perfectly that sport has always been a highly gendered social sphere, because men's control of female physical activity has been at the heart of masculine hegemony. Thus, women were denied the right to engage in physical exercise for different reasons, such as, the alleged

10   *Germany as a natural experiment*

'weakness' of the female bodies, detrimental effects on female fertility, chastity, or threats to the 'natural order' of the sexes (e.g., Messner, 1992; Pfister, 1993). In Germany, such reservations prevailed, even in the inter-war era, during which female participation in sport was rising (Pfister, 2002).

Female participation in soccer has been proven to be particularly contested as the sport has been strongly linked to hegemonic ideals of masculinity. Hence, when the English Football Association (FA) banned women's soccer in 1921, after female soccer teams had enjoyed a tremendous popularity during the war and the first inter-war years, it did so due to a mix of pseudo-scientific concerns about soccer's impact on women's health and fertility and reservations against an erosion of traditional gender roles (see Jacobs, 2004; Williams, 2014). The objections against women's participation in soccer might have been even stronger in Germany because the specific conditions for the sports' diffusion created particularly strong ties to masculinity (see also Pfister, 2008).

When soccer started migrating to Germany, the sport was met by fierce resistance of the patriotic German gymnastics ('Turnen') movement. The movement had played a decisive role in the patriotic upheaval of the nineteenth century, which eventually resulted in the founding of the German Empire in 1871. In contrast to English sports, Turnen did not emphasize record-seeking and competition but intended to develop the physical and moral powers of the Germans through joint practice of gymnastics. Notwithstanding its liberal origins, the bourgeois Turnen movement became increasingly conservative after the German unification in 1871 and perceived Turnen as the only legitimate national physical activity within the German Empire (Krüger, 1996). Accordingly, soccer was denounced as an English sport and a degraded form of physical activity (Langewiesche, 1990; Eisenberg, 1997), and, as a consequence, became only accepted after the sport had adapted to the militaristic cultural climate of the German Empire and was given a military habit, even to the extent where German soccer enthusiasts employed militaristic language for translating soccer terms (see Koch, 1895). Eventually, soccer received a decisive boost when it was made an element of military training because the military leadership regarded the autonomously acting soccer player to represent a role model for modern soldiers (Eisenberg, 1997: 101–102). Therefore, soccer became strongly linked to traditional ideas of masculinity. As noted by Selmer (2004), due to its successful adaptation to the political and cultural climate within the German Empire, soccer experienced a fast rise from a leisure activity of the emerging middle classes to a 'combat' sport and mass entertainment. By the end of the World War I, soccer had become

Germany as a natural experiment 11

Germany's national sport, starting to inspire patriotic feelings among the male population (Pfister, 2006).

Due to its strong ties to hegemonic ideas of masculinity, female participation in soccer was for a long time unthinkable in Germany. In the German Empire, *any* female participation in physical activity was controversial so the spectrum of sport for women was rather small (Pfister, 1980, 2003). The Turnen movement did initially not include girls and women. Only due to growing concerns about the detrimental health effects of female physical inactivity in particular on fertility, some participation of girls and women in gymnastics was finally accepted in Imperial Germany—yet only under strict regulations concerning 'indecent' practices (Pfister, 1980). After the Empire had collapsed, the Weimar Republic catalyzed a modernization of gender roles epitomized in the image of the 'new woman'. The 'new woman' was vaguely associated with fitness and physical activity (Becker, 1994). However, whereas female pioneers accomplished extraordinary things in traditional male sports during the inter-war years (Pfister, 1980: 33–34), the 'new woman' was certainly not representative for the everyday reality of the majority of German women (Becker, 1994). Moreover, the participation of women in competitive sports continued to be controversially discussed in the Weimar era for reasons of female health, in particular fertility, chastity, and fears of masculinization (Pfister, 1980).

These strong reservations applied in particular to soccer, due to its characterization as a combat sport. Conservative sport officials outright opposed women's participation in soccer. Yet, even the socialist Workers' Gymnastic and Sport Association (Arbeiter-, Turn- und Sportbund—ATSB), which encouraged female sport participation in general, had substantial reservations (Hoffmann & Nendza, 2006: 27). Thus, in contrast to Great Britain, France, Sweden, and Austria, women's soccer did not enjoy a boom in inter-war Germany. Certainly, some women played soccer. However, the first official women's soccer club was established as late as 1930 and survived only for a year (Hoffmann & Nendza, 2006: 28).

When Adolf Hitler assumed power in 1933, the conditions for women's soccer further worsened, as the aim of the National Socialists was to restore traditional gender roles. Hence, the DFB (Deutscher Fußballbund) issued an informal ban on women's soccer in 1936, claiming that the combat character of the sports was incompatible with the female nature (Hennies & Meuren, 2011: 15; Holsten & Wörner, 2011). Furthermore, the Nazis exploited the links between masculinity and soccer and intensified them by turning the men's national team into a symbol for German superiority and determination to win the war

12 Germany as a natural experiment

(Havemann, 2005: 225–226; Oswald, 2008: 147–150). Thus it was that a German women's soccer movement could only emerge after the end of World War II. However, both Germanys discriminated against women's soccer—although for different reasons and with different outcomes.

Women's soccer in West Germany: Reinforcing masculine hegemony

In West Germany, the links between patriotism, masculinity, and soccer became even stronger after the West German national team won the 1954 FIFA World Cup. The unexpected victory symbolized West Germany's recovery from the disastrous defeat in World War II and turned the men's national soccer team into one of the few uncontested national icons (Brüggemeier, 2004). Moreover, the conservative postwar social climate in West Germany was very unfavorable for female attempts to enter masculine spheres. After the Nazis' 'total war' effort had required higher female labor force participation, West German social conservatism aimed at restoring traditional gender roles. Women were relegated to unpaid homemaking and men to breadwinning (Rosenfeld et al., 2004: 104). In addition, once more, pseudo-scientific evidence, such as the famous treatise on soccer by Dutch sport physician Frederik Jacobus Johannes Buytendijk (1953), supported ideas of a general female ineptitude to play soccer and detrimental effects of the sports on women's health (Pfister, 2006).

So when the West German Football Association (DFB) issued a formal ban on women's football in July 1955, the officials followed as much the social conservative *zeitgeist* as they did a football-specific tradition of gender discrimination. The ban argued that women's soccer posed threats to female health and violated standards of decency and aesthetics. Thus, DFB clubs were denied the right to form a women's soccer team (Hoffmann & Nendza, 2006: 47). However, the ban did not stop female soccer enthusiasts from playing, even in the face of persistent media ridicule. To some extent, women's soccer turned into a domain for commercial entrepreneurs keen to exploit male voyeurism (see also Herzog, 2018). In 1957, Fortuna Düsseldorf was founded as a barnstorming team, that is, the team traveled to stage exhibition games. After such women's soccer events attracted substantial audiences, the DFB even tried to force municipalities to stop renting their sports grounds to commercial entrepreneurs. Emphasizing constitutional provisions on gender equality, the municipalities refused to do so and so the barnstorming of female soccer teams could continue (Hoffmann & Nendza, 2006: 57; Hennies & Meuren, 2011: 17–18). The pressure

Germany as a natural experiment 13

on the DFB to lift the ban on women's soccer substantially increased in the late 1960s in the wake of the changes of the sociocultural climate (Brändle & Koller, 2002: 221–222). Women's soccer enthusiasts started joining 'ordinary' soccer clubs and some clubs and state soccer associations tacitly accepted their membership (Hennies & Meuren, 2011: 39–41; Herzog, 2018). International developments further served to improve the prospects for women's soccer in West Germany. Many European soccer associations (FAs) had already accepted women's soccer. Moreover, rivalling international federations had formed and an unofficial World Cup was organized in Italy, which drew large crowd numbers in 1970. DFB and UEFA alike became worried that if they maintained their hostile stance toward women's soccer, they would lose control over the emerging grass-roots movement and eventually provoke organizational secession. Hence, UEFA started requesting its member FAs to address all issues of women's soccer in 1970. Finally, the DFB lifted its ban in 1970 in response to domestic as well as international developments (Pfister, 2003, 2006; Hoffmann & Nendza, 2006; Hennies & Meuren, 2011). As suggested by Herzog (2018), the lift of the ban on women's soccer was part of a more general strategy to open up soccer clubs for families and more diverse age and social groups.

Even though women's soccer certainly did not become a priority for the DFB, its incorporation into the association's structures proved highly beneficial and gave the sport a decisive boost (Pfister, 2001). In 1974, the first German championship was organized. Three years later, the DFB created a committee for women's soccer so that the sports gained some organizational representation. The committee started to develop a deliberate policy for girls' and women's soccer. In the 1980/1981 season, a national cup competition was introduced, and, from the 1985/1986 season on, regional leagues were organized. Finally, a national league with two divisions was formed in 1990. In 1982, the DFB created the women's national soccer team after the association had been invited to participate in an unofficial World Cup in 1981. Since no national team existed, a club team was delegated, which surprisingly won the tournament. In the aftermath, the national women's soccer team became the sport's most visible outlet, particularly after the 1989 European Competition for Women's Football (Hennies & Meuren, 2011: 135–140). The event hosted in West Germany marked a decisive milestone for women's soccer. For the first time, an entire women's soccer match was broadcast on West German TV. The sports was given a further boost when the German team surprisingly won the competition (Hoffmann & Nendza, 2006; Hennies & Meuren, 2011).[2]

14   *Germany as a natural experiment*

The status of women's soccer within the DFB improved further under the presidency of Theo Zwanziger (2004–2012). Zwanziger initiated programs for promoting girls' and women's soccer (Vaupel, 2014; Staab, 2017). The strategic turn represents, to a certain extent, a response to secular changes in gender roles, partly inspired by demographic changes, which were deemed to decrease men's membership figures in the long run (DFB, 2013; see also Wopp, 2007; Klein et al., 2012). Notwithstanding these efforts, soccer has remained a masculine sport. Girls and women account for only 15.9 percent of the 6.97 million DFB members and a considerable share of these female soccer club members might also not participate in soccer but may do so in other sports (DOSB, 2016).

Women's soccer in East Germany: Irrelevant for the Olympic medal record

At first glance, the prerequisites for women's soccer seemed to be more favorable in East Germany. Not only was gender equality an official goal of the socialist regime, female sport participation was also encouraged as a means to preserve work capacity (Budde, 2000). In addition, female athletes accounted to a considerable degree for East Germany's athletic success on the international stage—even though this success reflected the ruthless use of doping (Noland & Stahler, 2016). Nevertheless, East Germany failed to achieve gender equality in sport. East German women were strongly under-represented in sporting organizations and participated less in popular sports than West German women. Pfister (2002) provides a number of potential explanations for low female participation. In general, East German sport policymaking was heavily focused on elite sports while popular sport was dramatically under-resourced (Balbier, 2007; Dennis & Grix, 2012). Furthermore, even the supply of popular sport dedicated to traditional competitive sport, left little room for social or health motivated participation. Hence, East German popular sports failed to cater to the needs of many women.

These factors are also relevant for explaining why soccer remained a particularly gendered sports. A decisive factor for the marginalization of women's soccer was that the sport was irrelevant for the Olympic medal record, which was a top priority for East German sport policymaking (Balbier, 2007). In 1969, the politburo of the East German communist party decided to concentrate state subsidies on such sports that promised a high return on investments in terms of Olympic medals (see Teichler, 2002: 561–568). The elite sports resolution ('Leistungssportbeschluss') defined the following aims in 1969:

> Defending membership among the leading nations in international sports at the Summer Olympics
> Membership among the 10 best nations at the Winter Olympics
> Placements before West Germany at international championships in most of the supported summer and winter sports.
> (Politbüro des Zentralkomitees, 1998 [1969]: 567)

For achieving these aims, the resolution demanded a concentration of efforts on sports that promised a high return on investments in terms of Olympic medals. Thus, the GDR focused on individual sports that were regularly included in the Olympic Games; other sports faced severe cuts in public spending and participation was discouraged (Reinartz, 1999). The decision created a dichotomy in the East German sports system between highly subsidized elite sports ('Sport I') and lower priority sports ('Sport II'). The resolution implied that a team sport without any significant international competition, such as women's soccer, was automatically given only a low priority.[3]

Since East German sports officials were also not interested in losing female athletic talent to women's soccer (Hoffmann & Nendza, 2006: 137), the East German soccer association only hesitantly accepted girls' and women's soccer in response to uncontrolled grass-roots activities. As East German citizens did not enjoy the right to form voluntary grass-roots sport clubs, women's soccer enthusiasts had to rely on the support from company sports associations ('Betriebssportgemeinschaft—BSG'). Although the BSGs were subject to political pressure to focus on competitive sport (Tegelbeckers, 2003), some East German BSGs started supporting women's soccer. In 1968, the first East German women's soccer team was created under the auspices of the BSG 'Empor Dresden' (Linne, 2011: 39; see Chapter 2).

Nevertheless, women's soccer was not even classified as 'Sport II' but as 'leisure sports' ('Freizeit- und Erholungssport—FES') implying that the sport was not entitled to have regular competitions (Linne, 2011: 37). Being considered a non-elite leisure activity meant, among other things, that the sport did not receive much state subsidy and was denied the right to form a national level league. When the East German soccer association finally allowed for some form of national competition in 1978, women's soccer was not granted a full national league due to cost concerns. Accordingly, the competition was not called a national championship but 'determination of best team' ('Bestenermittlung') (Hennies & Meuren, 2011: 180). Although the country even fell behind the development of women's soccer in other Eastern European countries, the neglect for the sport continued until the peaceful revolution

16 *Germany as a natural experiment*

of 1989. Public subsidies remained very low until reunification and an East German women's national soccer team was not created before 1990. Due to the collapse of the socialist regime in the wake of the peaceful revolution, the team played only once (for more detail, see Linne, 2011, 2014).

To summarize so far: the development of girls' and women's soccer in East Germany lagged substantially behind West Germany at the time of reunification (Pfister, 2003, 2006; Linne, 2011, 2014). Accordingly, as with other societal domains in reunified Germany, women's soccer is characterized by two different and partly contradictory institutional legacies. On the one hand, the conditions for girls' and women's soccer seemed to be more favorable in West Germany. On the other hand, East Germany was by far the more gender-equal society. Therefore, the case of reunified Germany is highly instructive with regard to the question of which institutional legacy is ultimately more decisive for the development of girls' and women's soccer.

As already indicated, persistent East German legacies have been found in a number of policy domains (Svallfors, 2010; Bauernschuster & Rainer, 2011). Thus, reunified Germany strongly supported the idea that policies represent political forces in their own right, which shape future policy dynamics and influence public opinion (Soss & Schramm, 2007; Jacobs & Weaver, 2015). According to Soss and Schramm (2007: 113):

> Policies can set political agendas and shape identities and interests. They can influence beliefs about what is possible, desirable, and normal. They can alter conceptions of citizenship and status. They can channel or constrain agency, define incentives, and redistribute resources. They can convey cues that define, arouse, or pacify constituencies.

The idea that public policies shape not only the capacities, interests, and beliefs of political elites but also those of the general public has been decisively promoted by scholars of welfare policies (Campbell, 2012). Thus, Pierson (1993) claimed that many policies have 'resource' and 'interpretive' effects on target populations that alter their capacities and interests. Policies not only create constituencies, which benefit from them and, by implication, have a vested interest in maintaining them, policies may also institutionalize and legitimize certain norms, which can affect citizen's belief systems (Svallfors, 1997, 2006, 2010; Andreß & Heien 2001; Mau, 2004).

The specific mechanisms behind policy feedback can be diverse and policy domain-specific (Soss & Schramm, 2007; Gangle & Ziefle, 2015).

Scholars of women's soccer have already suggested that government policies are decisive for the development of women's soccer, either as support for the elite level (Jinxia & Mangan, 2002; Manzenreiter & Horne, 2007; Hong, 2012) or as specific leisure policies for girls and young women (Scraton et al., 1999). Not surprisingly, scholars have shown that the—often hostile—stance toward women's soccer adopted by soccer associations also plays a key role (Williams, 2003; Tate, 2013; Dunn, 2016). In addition, scholars have suggested media can influence the popularity of women's soccer (Jinxia & Mangan, 2002). In the case of girls' and women's soccer in Germany, the resource effects of communist sports policies should be almost self-evident: Due to under-resourcing, women's soccer in East Germany had to struggle to attract talent and develop a professional structure. In terms of interpretive effects, East German sports policies were even more likely to solidify public perception of women's soccer as a recreational activity, not qualifying as a serious elite sport.

The themes of the book

This book is set out to examine the 'future of soccer is feminine' *leitmotif*, using Germany as an empirical example. At its most basic meaning, the 'future of soccer is feminine' thesis implies a trend toward more female soccer participation as well as the growing popularity of women's soccer. In general, Germany seems to provide quite favorable conditions for the development of women's soccer. Moreover, the modernization of German family and labor regulations, as well as gender-role attitudes in particular among younger Germans, should work in favor of women's soccer. However, several institutional legacies might mitigate further growth and acceptance of girls' and women's soccer. The differences and tensions in East and West German gender regimes raise the question of whether they have left lasting legacies on the development and popularity of women's soccer. Furthermore, in case such legacies exist, it is of interest whether there is a trend toward convergence. Thus, the book tries to take on the challenge as posed by Valenti et al. (2018) to identify, model, and test the contextual and sport-related factors that drive girls' and women's soccer development. By tracing the impact of policy legacies, the book tries to contribute to a more general theory on the development of girls' and women's soccer by emphasizing institutional factors to be taken into account.

The book is organized as follows: The second chapter will examine the development of grass-roots girls' and women's soccer in a number of German state associations. The third chapter analyzes demand for

18 *Germany as a natural experiment*

first-tier women's professional soccer in Germany. The fourth chapter studies the popularity of the women's national soccer team as the sport's most visible outlet. Chapter Five aims to draw more general conclusions concerning the future of girls' and women's soccer.

The methods of the book

In order to address the themes just outlined, this book employs a strict quantitative approach. By doing so, the book aims to fill a gap in the empirical literature. As the integrative review of Valenti et al. (2018) has shown, most of the research on women's soccer has employed qualitative approaches. This research has brought about important insights on which the book eclectically builds. Although research agendas have become more diversified, many scholars have followed the theoretical guidance of Scraton et al. (1999: 99) who characterized access to women's soccer as the political outcome of a liberal-feminist discourse centering on equal opportunities, socialization practices and legal or institutional reform. By now, there exists an impressive stock of well-crafted studies on the development of women's soccer in different national and cultural contexts (e.g., Lopez, 1997; Jinxia & Mangan, 2002; Pfister, 2003; Williams, 2003; Hall, 2004; Liston, 2006; Manzenreiter & Horne, 2007; Manzenreiter, 2008; Pelak, 2010; Da Costa, 2014). Whereas a common theme of many contributions is that women's soccer represents a battlefield for the negotiation of gender roles (e.g., Manzenreiter, 2008), the in-depth and contextualized insights into the development of women's soccer are difficult to systematize into a more general framework for understanding the development of women's soccer.

Stricter quantitative research is needed for advancing the academic and practical knowledge about girls' and women's soccer, for two reasons. First, studying detailed and longitudinal data on sports development can serve as a precaution against too optimistic scenarios regarding the future of women's soccer. Second, valid insights into empirical variety and the explanatory power of quantitative models indicate scope for discretionary agency, that is, unexploited opportunities to further promote girls' and women's soccer.

Hence, the current book complements existing qualitative accounts. Moreover, it also indicates the shortcomings of existing quantitative and qualitative research. On several occasions, the individual chapters emphasize that deeper and context-sensitive analyses of association and club policies and their effects are needed in order to give valid policy advice. As Valenti et al. (2018) have stressed, future research has to analyze the evolution of women's football from managerial and business

Germany as a natural experiment 19

perspectives. Hence, ultimately the analyses illustrate that ideally quantitative and qualitative approaches should complement each other.

Notes

1 The only exception is Torgler (2008) who did not control for gender equality.
2 Even the DFB was taken by surprise and hastily organized a coffee and table service as a bonus for the players.
3 It is important to note that the first FIFA Women's World Cup was organized in 1991 and the first Olympic women's soccer tournament in 1996.

2 The development of girls' and women's grass-roots soccer

Introduction

Reunified Germany enjoys a reputation for representing a natural experiment for studying the impact of policy legacies because the reunification of 1990 placed two very different societies under the West German regime, after 40 years of division. The transfer of West German institutions has since then raised the question of how East German attitudes and behaviors would adapt (Konietzka & Kreyenfeld, 2002; Lee et al., 2007; Bauernschuster & Rainer, 2011; Hanel & Riphan, 2011). While girls' and women's grass-roots soccer faced low acceptance and substantial reservations in both parts of divided Germany, these reservations differed with respect to both, the motives behind them, and the measures adopted to enforce them. As a result, the trajectories along which girls' and women's soccer developed differed in both Germanys.

Hence, after the West German DFB had lifted its ban on women's soccer in 1970, the sport started benefitting from the association's professional approach. Even though girls' and women's soccer did not become a top priority of the DFB, the association initiated several promotional programs in order to inspire more grass-roots participation by girls and women in DFB membership clubs (Pfister, 2001). In contrast, girls' and women's soccer remained strongly marginalized in East Germany because it was irrelevant for the Olympic medal record (Linne, 2011, 2014). Girls' and women's soccer received only limited financial and organizational support. Furthermore, the East German communists opposed the German tradition of state-free clubs and associations as much as the Nazis did (Luh, 2003) but were much more successful in gaining control over grass-roots sports. Thus, the development of grass-roots girls' and women's soccer was primarily left to the discretion of company sports organizations (Betriebssportgemeinschaften—BSGs), which had little reason to invest in marginal sports with uncertain elite prospects (Tegelbeckers, 2003; see 'Institutional legacies' below). Yet,

Girls' and women's grass-roots soccer 21

BSGs, in particular those with higher spending power, also enjoyed some discretion, which enabled some women's soccer enthusiasts to found women's teams. Thus, the first East German women's soccer team was established through an initiative of the Bulgarian student Wladimir Zwetkow, who managed to convince the officials of its merits, under the auspices of the BSG 'Empor Dresden' in 1968 (Linne, 2011: 39). Three years later, the most successful women's club, 'Turbine Potsdam', was also created by a BSG (Hoffmann & Nendza, 2006: 137). Given the strong reservations felt by East German sports officials, it should not come as a surprise that the number of competitive teams remained low (Hoffmann & Nendza, 2006: 140) and the development of girls' and women's grass-roots soccer in East Germany lagged substantially in comparison to West Germany at the time of reunification (Pfister, 2003, 2006; Linne, 2011, 2014).

This chapter traces the development of grass-roots girls' and women's soccer in post-reunification Germany. According to the 'future of soccer is feminine' *leitmotif* of the book, the chapter will first examine whether participation in grass-roots girls' and women's soccer is increasing. In addition, the chapter exploits Germany's character as a natural experiment for studying the impact of macro-social conditions and institutional legacies on sports development. East Germany shows a combination of unfavorable macro-economic and institutional legacies, which are likely to serve as barriers to further growth in girls' and women's soccer. In order to conceptualize how contextual factors affect the population of girls' and women's soccer teams, the chapter combines eclectically on theoretical and methodological ideas from sport geography and organizational ecology.

Girls' and women's grass-roots sports as spatially constrained activities

The pioneer of sport geography, John Bale (2003), has emphasized that sport has to be understood as a spatially constrained activity with its own space–time geography (O'Reilly et al., 2015). There exist diverse approaches to studying the spatial dimension of sport (van Ingen, 2003; Ilies et al., 2014). In accordance with the key questions outlined, the approach employed here will focus on the impact of macro-social factors and institutional legacies on sports development. In order to theorize how these factors affect the population of girls' and women's soccer, insights into sport geography will be combined with basic concepts from organizational ecology (Hannan & Freeman, 1977, 1984, 1989; Carroll & Hannan, 2004). This particular approach of organization theory

22   *Girls' and women's grass-roots soccer*

represents a general macro-sociological theory intended to explain the development of organizational populations. The approach focuses on contextual causes that produce variations in organizational founding and failure rates over time by influencing opportunity structures for founders and resource constraints for existing organizations (Baum & Amburgey, 2002).

The impact of macro-social conditions on the spatial organization of sports

Regarding the impact of macro-social factors on the developments of sport, scholars of sport geography have emphasized that secular economic changes, in particular 'rural restructuring', exert a substantial impact on sport provision, activity, and participation (Tonts & Atherley, 2005; Oncescu, 2015). Building on Hoggart and Paniagua (2001), Jacquelyn Oncescu (2015: 83–84) has defined 'rural restructuring' as referring to changes in the rural economy that are undermining the social and economic viability of rural community life. The economic changes involve capital outflows, job losses, and out-migration in favor of (more) urban regions. Thus, rural restructuring has far-reaching implications for physical activity and sport.

As Oncescu (2015) has emphasized, rural restructuring serves to reduce recreational opportunities and participation as well as financial capacities and support for recreation at the family and community levels. In particular, the out-migration of young people makes it more difficult for municipalities to sustain service delivery and infrastructure since the (fixed) costs for delivering recreation services are higher in rural areas because of geographic dispersion, smaller tax bases, and the reduced ability to generate revenue (Buchanan & Buchanan, 1987). Furthermore, rural restructuring results not only in out-migration but often forces remaining families into commuting, which serves to reduce their financial and time resources (Oncescu, 2015). By implication, rural restructuring leads to a decrease in recreation and leisure opportunities, which is also detrimental for the creation of social capital (Tonts, 2005; Atherley, 2006; Oncescu & Robertson, 2010; Oncescu, 2015).

These insights seem to be highly relevant for the geography of girls' and women's soccer in Germany. First, Germany faces persistent trends of urbanization and rural restructuring, which are related to far-reaching demographic changes, such as, a low fertility rate and persistent immigration. As a result of these trends, German metropolitan areas will be confronted with population growth and increasing multi-ethnicity, whereas rural areas face depopulation, ageing, youth

Girls' and women's grass-roots soccer 23

out-migration and threats to socio-economic viability (e.g., BMI, 2014a, 2014b). In general, urbanization and rural restructuring serve to increase geographical disparity in leisure and recreational opportunities (Tonts, 2005; Atherley, 2006; Rosso, 2008; Oncescu & Robertson, 2010; Oncescu, 2015). Accordingly, German rural municipalities struggle to sustain service delivery and sport infrastructure (Leibert & Golinski, 2017). Since German municipality schools provide much of the infrastructure for local sports clubs, youth out-migration—and the following inevitable school closures—will result in the loss of key sport facilities (Hübner, 2008). Urban or metropolitan areas enjoy, in contrast, substantial advantages in terms of sport infrastructure, such as a higher variety of sports facilities and shorter travel distances (Hoekman et al., 2016a, 2016b). The superior infrastructure provision is likely to increase sports participation (Wicker et al., 2009; Hallmann et al., 2012; O'Reilly et al., 2015).

With regard to a potential East–West divide in Germany, it is relevant that rural restructuring and out-migration are much more pronounced in East Germany due to economic transformation from a centrally planned to a market economy (Sinn & Sinn, 1992; Burda & Hunt, 2001; Hunt, 2006). When the monetary and economic union between West and East Germany became effective on July 1, 1990, the state-directed East German economy was ill prepared to face global competition, which immediately started. East German industry suffered from outdated capital stock and an uncompetitive structure of output. As estimated by Akerlof et al. (1991), only one-fifth of East Germany's industry was competitive at the 1:1 conversion rate between the East German Mark and the Deutsche Mark, which had been politically determined. Thus, the monetary union resulted in a dramatic labor cost squeeze, which was further aggravated by substantial wage increases bargained by West German union officials who tried to prevent more intense competition in the labor market (Heiland, 2004).

This economic disruption or 'shock transformation' resulted in one of the worst and sharpest depressions in European history, which culminated in deindustrialization and high unemployment rates (Akerlof et al., 1991; Burda & Hunt, 2001; Hunt, 2006). Although generous welfare transfers raised living standards in East Germany, de-industrialization and high unemployment rates catalyzed several waves of out-migration to West Germany as well as an abrupt drop in fertility rates (Witte & Wagner, 1995). Due to de-industrialization and outmigration, East Germany has lost its future work force (Uhlig, 2008). Nowadays, most parts of East Germany lack the industrial agglomerations or clusters needed to generate sufficient employment

24   *Girls' and women's grass-roots soccer*

opportunities to keep or attract well-educated people. Whereas East Germany represented a highly industrialized region before reunification, it has now the lowest rate of industrial employment in Western Europe (Wiechmann & Pallagst, 2012). The East–West gap in economic development, which has been constantly reported by the federal government (BMWi, 2017), might be preserved rather than mitigated by the particular mix of policies employed to subsidize East Germany (Snower & Merkl, 2006), In any case, persistent out-migration is a broader phenomenon in East Germany, which threatens not only the viability of rural communities but has turned urban shrinkage into a broader phenomenon (Wiechmann & Pallagst, 2012).

These macro-social developments are likely to leave an impact on the development and spatial distribution of girls' and women's soccer. For theorizing these effects, the concept of an organizational niche as developed by organizational ecology appears to be particularly useful. An organizational niche consists of all those combinations of resource levels at which the population can survive and reproduce itself (Hannan & Freeman, 1977: 947). Organizational niches 'can represent mappings from organizational fitness to a diverse array of environmental properties, including tastes of consumers, potential employees, availability of various kinds of input (e.g., human and financial capital), and legal and regulatory regimes' (Hannan et al., 2003: 314). Here it is assumed that macro-social trends affect the organizational niche width for girls' and women's soccer, which can be defined by the target audience of an organizational population.

As McPherson (1983) has emphasized, voluntary organizations target limited segments of communities primarily defined by the socio-demographic characteristics of their members. Therefore, many organizational niches can be identified via the positioning of an organization in a more dimensional socio-demographic space (Bruggeman et al., 2012; Barroso et al. 2016). Such a socio-demographic version of the niche concept corresponds with a 'subcultural' approach to leisure activities, which emphasizes that structural factors such as socio-economic status and neighborhood residence continue to shape leisure activities (Shildrick, 2006; Shildrick & MacDonald, 2006). Here, it suffices to realize that rural restructuring and persistent East German out-migration are likely to substantially shrink the target audience for girls' and women's soccer. Moreover, as in other countries (Edlund, 2005), out-migration in Germany is age- and sex-selective. More precisely, young people and women are more likely to leave rural regions and East Germany than men (Leibert, 2016). This female outmigration appears to be driven by the persistence of traditional gender roles in

Girls' and women's grass-roots soccer 25

rural regions and the male domination of the public sphere and social associations (Leibert & Wiest, 2016).

Institutional legacies and the spatial organization of sports

As discussed in the introductory chapter, in addition to rather unfavorable macro-social conditions, East German policy legacies are likely to negatively affect the development of girls' and women's soccer. Throughout this book, policies are understood as political forces in their own right, which shape future policy dynamics and influence public attitudes and perceptions (Soss & Schramm, 2007; Jacobs & Weaver, 2015). For understanding the impact of East German sports policies on girls' and women's soccer it is useful to build on Paul Pierson's (1993) famous distinction between 'resource' and 'interpretive' effects of policies.

With regard to 'resource' effects, Pierson (1993) has argued that the provision and allocation of political and material resources by public policies serves not only to create incentives for existing social interest groups but also to create such constituencies in the first place. In consequence, these constituencies develop a vested interest in maintaining these policies and are likely to act as political lobby groups. Concerning 'interpretive' effects, Pierson (1993) initially focused on cognitive processes, such as policy-learning. Subsequent research has more strongly emphasized that policies serve to institutionalize and legitimize certain norms, which might affect citizen's belief systems. Thus, welfare policies have been found to have left a persistent effect on perceptions of social justice by the general public (Svallfors, 1997, 2006, 2010; Andreß & Heien 2001; Mau, 2004).

For girls' and women's soccer, two East German policy legacies seem to be of particular relevance, that is, the institutional weakness of the voluntary sports sector in general and the neglect of women's soccer in particular. With regard to a persistent weakness of the voluntary sports sector, it is important that, notwithstanding the lip service paid to a 'sports for all' policy, the East German sports system was heavily focused on elite sport, and popular sport was dramatically under-resourced (Krebs, 1995; Teichler, 2002; Dennis & Grix, 2012). Moreover, in order to guarantee political control over citizens' leisure activities, the East German communists abolished the 'bourgeois' system of voluntary sport clubs and replaced it with so-called 'sport communities' (Sportgemeinschaften—SGs). The SGs were not only subject to political control but also heavily dependent on external funding as they were not allowed to increase their membership fees beyond very low

26 *Girls' and women's grass-roots soccer*

thresholds. Since these low membership fees could not sustain the SGs, popular sport was mostly funded and organized by company sports associations (Betriebssportgemeinschaften—BSGs). The willingness of the parent companies to subsidize popular sports varied substantially with the effect that popular sports in East Germany often remained under-resourced (Tegelbeckers, 2003).

Reunification brought about an immense change in the governance of East German popular sport. As in other domains, East Germany was compelled to adopt West German sports institutions, which—since World War II—have relied on voluntary organizations, that is, sports clubs organized as democratic membership associations. These clubs are free to choose their supply according to their members' preferences but do also carry the main burden of providing the funding for this particular supply (Horch, 1983). The voluntary sports sector has been extremely successful in including a substantial share of the West German population (Breuer & Feiler, 2017). Even though the East German statistics are notoriously unreliable, it is incontrovertible that the politically controlled SGs and BSGs had failed to inspire a similar level of mass participation (Tegelbeckers, 2003). The already unfavorable institutional prerequisites for popular sports in East Germany worsened after reunification. Due to deindustrialization and plant closures, many BSGs ceased to exist because their low membership fees did not suffice to sustain them. Moreover, as Tonts and Atherley (2005: 142) have emphasized, 'processes of restructuring have the potential to fragment or degrade the associated social networks'. Accordingly, the substantial out-migration from East Germany destroyed the very social capital needed to sustain volunteer organizations such as sports clubs. Thus, a problematic institutional legacy of East German sports policies is a general weakness of a strong voluntary sports movement. According to the official membership statistics, 31 percent of the West German population are members of a sport club, but only 16 percent of the East German population (see DOSB, 2018: 12).

In addition to these generally unfavorable conditions for volunteer sports, East German sports policies came with particular problematic resource and interpretive effects for girls' and women's soccer. As indicated several times, the sport was only reluctantly accepted by East German soccer officials in response to decentralized activities by some BSGs (for more detail, see Linne, 2011, 2014). Yet, women's soccer was never classified as an elite sport, which implied that the sport did not receive much public subsidy (Hennies & Meuren, 2011). Moreover, the particular governance of the East German sports sector made it unattractive for BSGs to dedicate resources to marginal sports, such as

Girls' and women's grass-roots soccer 27

girls' and women's soccer. On the one hand, the BSGs were subject to continuous (and unrealistic) expectations concerning increases in membership figures. On the other hand, even popular sports in East Germany were expected to focus on traditional competitive sport (Tegelbeckers, 2003). Finally, any serious efforts to promote grass-roots girls' and women's soccer were impeded as girls under 16 were not allowed to participate so as to avoid wasting their potential for athletic talent (Hennies & Meuren, 2011: 179–180). Hence, it is not surprising that, due to persistent under-resourcing and neglect, girls' and women's soccer in East Germany had to struggle to attract talent and develop professional structures. The pioneers of East German women's soccer had little illusions about the prospects of their sport under the communist regime. As Bernd Schröder (2017: 52), long-time manager and coaching legend of the East German team 'Turbine Potsdam', remembered:

> Knowing the basic principles of GDR sport policies, it was quite clear to me and my fellow campaigners [for women's soccer] that progressive development and support was only realistic in case women's soccer became Olympic.

The unfavorable resource effects materialized in a blatant underdevelopment of women's soccer in East Germany at the time of reunification (Pfister, 2003, 2006; Linne, 2011, 2014).

In addition to those unfavorable resource effects, East German sports policies were—even more than in the West—likely to solidify a public perception of women's soccer as a recreational activity, not qualifying as a serious elite sport. Hence, a lasting interpretive effect of East German sports policies might be that East German sports organizations might dismiss the claims for resources made by girls' and women's soccer as not as legitimate as the claims made by the more traditional competitive sports.

These insights come with implications for the second niche dimension considered here, that is, niche overlap and resource competition. Organizational ecology argues that if the niche of an organizational population heavily overlaps with the niche of another population then resource competition can be intense (see Hannan et al., 2003). As argued, economic transformation and out-migration are likely to shrink the organizational niche for girls' and women's sport in rural regions in general and East Germany in particular. Moreover, economic transformation, rural restructuring and out-migration reduce financial capacities and support for recreation and sports opportunities at the community level. Thus, resources become increasingly scarce. As Rosso (2008) has

28 *Girls' and women's grass-roots soccer*

demonstrated, a lack of facilities, in particular, can represent a major obstacle for the development of girls' and women's soccer. Therefore, it seems likely that girls' and women's soccer is not only less developed in East Germany but also that the sport might also face persistent difficulties in successfully claiming the necessary resources.

In the light of these considerations, it seems trivial to expect an East–West gap in the geography of girls' and women's soccer. However, unfavorable macro-social conditions and institutional legacies make it conceivable that the East–West gap in the development of the sport even increases over time. On the one hand, the niche for girls' and women's soccer continues to decrease in East Germany. On the other hand, East German policy legacies are likely to further marginalize the sport under conditions of more intense competition over scarce resources. Finally, given persistent processes of rural restructuring and urbanization, girls' and women's soccer should be more of an urban phenomenon. The empirical section of this chapter tries to examine these ideas by following the standard methodological approaches of organizational ecology. Hence, first, the organizational population of grass-roots girls' and women's soccer will be studied by tracing the number of teams in German municipalities. Second, it will be examined whether team survival differs according to contextual factors.

Analyzing data on girls' and women's soccer

In order to trace the impact of macro-social factors and policy legacies, a unique dataset on girls' and women's grass-roots soccer in Germany, provided by the DFB, is analyzed (see Appendix). The fourth tier of competitive women's soccer represents the highest league level analyzed here. A particular advantage of using data on teams actually participating in league competitions is that they provide a more reliable picture of grass-roots girls' and women's soccer than membership figures. Since some soccer clubs offer a multitude of sports, membership data include not only passive club members but also members practicing sports other than soccer (Klein et al., 2012). Therefore, the member share and team share of all 21 state associations correlated only moderately in 2015 ($r = 0.582$; $p = 0.006$).

Unfortunately, not all DFB membership associations were willing to license their data. Therefore, the development of women's soccer could only be analyzed in 17 out of 21 state associations. The four associations not participating are the associations of Lower Rhine, Saxony, Westphalia, and Wuerttemberg. Nevertheless, state associations included here cover German regions of substantial socio-demographic

Girls' and women's grass-roots soccer 29

Figure 2.1 German state associations participating in the study

Note: Author's own depiction; the author is very grateful for the support of Marike Meijer.

and economic diversity. The dataset includes more than 80,000 valid entries on 'team seasons', that is, an observation on an individual soccer team in a distinct season for the period from 2005/2006 to 2015/2016. Figure 2.1 illustrates the geographical distribution of the state associations covered here.

By using postal codes, these team data could be linked to official municipality statistics conducted by the federal states. Unfortunately, as

30 *Girls' and women's grass-roots soccer*

discussed by Meier, Konjer and Nagm (2017), these data suffer from a number of limitations (see also Appendix). As the 'statistical resolution' is much higher for smaller municipalities than for larger municipalities, the 'city-states' Berlin, Bremen, and Hamburg had to be excluded from the multivariate analyses. Furthermore, the set of available statistical indicators differs across federal states. Finally, the official population figures in Germany have been heavily revised by the 2011 census (Christensen et al., 2015), which came with the rather unfavorable implication that advanced statistical analyses were primarily conducted for the period after 2011.

Notwithstanding these difficulties, two datasets could be constructed: A count dataset on the number of teams per municipality and a dataset on team survival. The first dataset has been constructed to study the organizational population of girls' and women's soccer teams by counting the *Number of adult teams per municipality* and the *Number of youth teams per municipality* referring to all U18 teams. The second dataset represents a dataset on team survival in which time-to-event, that is, time-to-team dissolution, serves as the dependent variable. The analyses are restricted to the period from the season 2005/2006 to 2015/2016. Accordingly, the data were left-truncated or left-censored. More precisely, for all teams, which were established before the 2005/2006 season, the actual date of founding is treated as unknown. Right-censoring occurs for teams which survive the 2015/2016 season.

The analyses try to control for the impact of macro-social factors and institutional legacies by including a number of control variables. Most importantly, the dummy variable *East* refers to the East German federal states and serves primarily as a proxy for institutional legacies. *County* represents a dummy variable for municipalities, which also enjoy a county status. With some reservations, the variable might be considered as a rough proxy for urbanity as such municipalities with county status represent either big cities or regional centers. *Inhabitants* refers to the total number of inhabitants divided by 1,000 residing in a municipality. *Density* measures local population density as inhabitants by square kilometer. As *Inhabitants* as well as *Density* are strongly right-skewed, they have been log-transformed (*lnInhabitants* and *lnDensity*). *Youth* represents the population share of municipality inhabitants younger than 15 years and *Age* the population share of municipality inhabitants older than 65 years. *Women* refers to the share of female inhabitants in a municipality. Demographic trends have been measured by *Relative Population Change* (see Appendix). In order to compensate for the lack of GDP data at the municipality level, the *Social insured share* serves as a proxy for local employment conditions.

Girls' and women's grass-roots soccer 31

The dataset on team survival includes additional characteristics of clubs and teams. In order to take into account the commitment of a club to girls' and women's soccer, *Teams per club* counts the total number of girls' and womens' teams in the respective clubs. *Relegation* represents a dummy variable for teams that were recently relegated. Vice versa, *Promotion* represents a dummy variable for recently promoted teams. *League* indicates the rank of the league in which the team was playing. Constructing one unified indicator for league membership proved difficult due to the diverse league structures in the state associations (Appendix). *Age class* indicates the age class in which the team is playing. The DFB distinguished the following age classes: Women older than 18 years, A Juniors ('U 18/U 19'), that is, girls of 17 or 18 years, B Juniors ('U 16/U 17'), that is, girls of 15 or 16 years, C Juniors ('U 14/U 15'), that is, girls of 13 or 14 years, D Juniors ('U 12/U 13'), that is, girls of 11 or 12 years, E Juniors ('U 10/U 11'), that is, girls of 9 or 10 years, F Juniors ('U 8/U 9'), that is, girls of 7 or 8 years, and, finally, G Juniors ('Bambini') referring to girls under 7 years. Moreover, in the survival dataset, *County* proved to be much more strongly associated with population size and density. Thus, *County* was considered to represent a valid proxy for urbanity. Accordingly, the survival data could be analyzed for the entire period from the 2005/2006 to the 2015/2016 season.

Stagnation and regional diversity

The visualization of the aggregate data shows that in contradiction to the 'future of soccer is feminine' claim, there is no growth trend in competitive girls' and women's soccer. After a peak in the 2008/2009 season, the total number of teams has almost continuously declined. However, over the entire ten-year period, the number of teams has increased by around 25 percent. The increase results mainly from the adult teams whose number was also not subject to a dramatic decline after the 2008/2009 season. Other age classes that experienced a total increase over the entire period, are E Junior teams (16 percent growth) and A Juniors, F Juniors and G Juniors, which did not exist in the 2005/2006 season. A total decline in team numbers is to be found for B Juniors (-18 percent), C Juniors (-5 percent) and D Juniors (-5 percent). Thus, the data show that, despite a long-term growth in girls' and women's soccer, the development of the sport stagnates. Furthermore, growth problems in lower age classes are evident (Figure 2.2).

Mapping the geographical distribution of girls' and women's soccer teams makes evident that a considerable number of East German

32 *Girls' and women's grass-roots soccer*

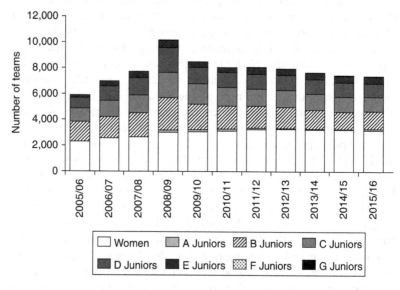

Figure 2.2 Number of women's and girls' teams in 17 German state associations

Note: Women: Women older than 18 years; A Juniors ('U 18/U 19'): girls of 17 or 18 years; B Juniors ('U 16/U 17'): girls of 15 or 16 years; C Juniors ('U 14/U 15'): girls of 13 or 14 years; D Juniors ('U 12/U 13'): girls of 11 or 12 years; E Juniors ('U 10/U 11'): girls of 9 or 10 years; F Juniors ('U 8/U 9'): girls of 7 or 8 years; G Juniors ('Bambini'): girls under 7 years.

municipalities hosts no girls' or women's teams at all, which is consistent with the theoretical expectations. However, there exists also a lot of 'blank space' in West German regions. Furthermore, the state association of Lower Saxony appears to represent a key region for girls' and women's soccer (Figure 2.3). The key indicators displayed in Table 3.3 provide further support for the general claim that East Germany is a more difficult environment for girls' and women's soccer. The East German state associations, that is, Brandenburg, Mecklenburg-West Pomerania, Saxony-Anhalt, and Thuringia, score particularly low in absolute team numbers and team density. Two of these state associations have even experienced a decline in team numbers over the entire period. However, in contradiction to the general idea that urban regions represent a more favorable environment for girls' and women's soccer, team density is not in general higher in the metropolitan city-states, that is, Berlin, Bremen, and Hamburg, but actually particularly low

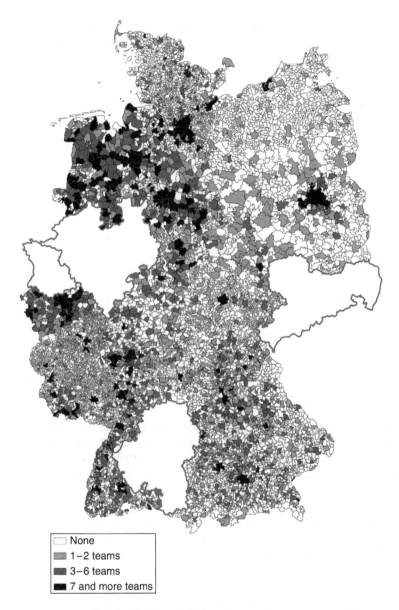

Figure 2.3 Spatial distribution of girl's and women's soccer across Germany

Source: Displayed is the total number of girls' and women's soccer teams per municipality. Author's own depiction; the author is very grateful for the support of Marike Meijer.

34 *Girls' and women's grass-roots soccer*

Table 2.1 The state of girls' and women's soccer in state associations

State association	Teams[a]	Density[b]	Tiers[c]	Survival time[d]	Increase[e]
East Germany					
Brandenburg	152	6.1	3	4.27	171%
Mecklenburg-West Pomerania	45	2.8	3	4.23	114%
Saxony-Anhalt	105	4.7	4	4.60	−7%
Thuringia	96	4.4	4	4.50	−11%
West Germany					
Baden	259	12.2	3	3.24	60%
Bavaria	1,585	12.3	7	4.02	32%
Berlin	229	6.5	3	4.54	68%
Bremen	69	12.4	4	3.94	35%
Hamburg	365	20.4	5	3.48	1%
Hesse	606	9.8	6	4.34	53%
Lower Saxony	1,975	24.9	6	3.49	9%
Middle Rhine	480	10.9	4	3.36	50%
Rhineland	257	15.4	3	3.01	82%
Saarland	124	12.5	4	3.31	3%
Schleswig-Holstein	351	12.3	4	3.15	−18%
South Baden	414	16.5	6	4.07	29%
South West Germany	212	9.2	3	4.04	57%

Note: a. Teams = Total number of teams; b. Density = Number of teams per 100,000 inhabitants; c. Tiers = Total number of tiers (leagues) in women age class; d. Survival time = Restricted mean survival time; e. Increase = Change in total number of teams from 2005/2006 to 2015/2016.

in Berlin. Moreover, the number of teams is highest in the two state associations, which cover rather large territories, that is, Bavaria and Lower Saxony (Table 2.1). Concerning regional differences in team survival, the Kaplan-Meier graph indicates that East German girls' and women's soccer teams face indeed higher risks of dissolution until the sixth season of their existence (Figure 2.4).

The multivariate analyses for the impact of macro-social conditions and institutional legacies on the number of teams per municipality employ methods for count data analyses. Accordingly, incidence rate ratios (IRRs) are displayed. IRRs greater than one indicate a higher probability that a municipality hosts a higher number of girls' and women's teams. By implication, IRRs less than one indicate a lower probability (Table 2.2).

The simple models for analyzing the number of teams per municipality indicate the existence of an East–West gap, which seems to particularly strong for youth teams (Models 1, 5, and 8). However,

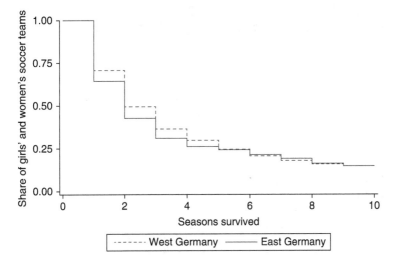

Figure 2.4 Team survival in German girls' and women's soccer

introducing interaction terms and a state association dummy serves to inflate the coefficients for the *East* dummy, which cease to be statistically significant at least for all models referring to adult team numbers (Models 2 to 4). Accordingly, it might be inferred that for women soccer teams, East–West differences are less important than differences between state associations. Yet, the coefficients for the East German state associations still suggest that East Germany performs worse when it comes to the number of adult teams per municipality. However, these effects are statistically not significant. In addition, some West German state associations, in particular Rhineland and South West, are significantly underperforming in comparison.

In contrast, the *East* effect seems to be more robust for the number of youth teams (see Models 5 and 7). Moreover, for the number of youth teams per municipality, two context conditions, that is, a higher youth share and a better population balance, play a significant stronger role in East Germany. This finding is consistent with the ideas on a detrimental impact of persistent out-migration on East German sports. Interestingly, when controlled for the general *East* effect, the East German state association of Brandenburg seems to be characterized by a significantly higher number of youth teams per municipality (Models 6 and 8). In addition, the two West German state associations of Rhineland and South West Germany are also characterized by significantly lower youth

Table 2.2 Analyzing girls' and women's soccer teams per municipality

Independent variables	Adult teams per municipality				Youth teams per municipality			
	Model 1	Model 2	Model 3	Model 4	Model 5	Model 6	Model 7	Model 8
East	0.615***	1.0×10^{33}	0.867	5.3×10^{30}	0.178***	3.2×10^{30}	0.108***	5.5×10^{27}
	(0.043)	(4.7×10^{34})	(0.139)	(2.4×10^{32})	(0.024)	(3.1×10^{32})	(0.033)	(5.4×10^{29})
lnInhabitants	2.898***	2.876***	2.723***	2.673***	3.410***	3.365***	3.226***	3.184***
	(0.058)	(0.062)	(0.065)	(0.070)	(0.089)	(0.088)	(0.099)	(0.098)
County status	0.524***	0.541**	0.811	0.542**	0.475***	0.296*	0.718*	0.426
	(0.045)	(0.123)	(0.096)	(0.120)	(0.051)	(0.156)	(0.101)	(0.233)
Women share	0.940***	0.936***	0.948**	0.944**	0.960	0.959	0.969	0.968
	(0.016)	(0.016)	(0.017)	(0.017)	(0.020)	(0.021)	(0.020)	(0.021)
Youth share	1.015	1.020	1.002	1.003	1.147***	1.142***	1.117***	1.112***
	(0.011)	(0.012)	(0.011)	(0.012)	(0.017)	(0.018)	(0.017)	(0.018)
Social share	1.014**	1.016**	1.011	1.014*	1.020**	1.022**	1.019*	1.021**
	(0.006)	(0.006)	(0.006)	(0.006)	(0.007)	(0.007)	(0.008)	(0.008)
Relative change	0.994	0.993	0.996	0.997	0.993	0.988	0.995	0.990
	(0.006)	(0.006)	(0.006)	(0.006)	(0.008)	(0.009)	(0.008)	(0.009)
Year	0.972***	0.976**	0.973***	0.974**	0.953***	0.953***	0.947***	0.947***
	(0.007)	(0.008)	(0.007)	(0.008)	(0.009)	(0.009)	(0.009)	(0.010)
East ×								
lnInhabitants		1.044		1.101		1.339		1.240
		(0.068)		(0.078)		(0.258)		(0.246)
County status		0.968		1.635		1.577		1.693
		(0.238)		(0.423)		(0.844)		(0.956)

Women share	1.038		1.026	1.247	1.269
	(0.069)		(0.070)	(0.190)	(0.194)
Youth share	1.030		1.058	1.125*	1.141*
	(0.033)		(0.034)	(0.058)	(0.060)
Social share	0.985		0.978	0.959	0.949
	(0.016)		(0.016)	(0.037)	(0.038)
Relative change	0.991		0.985	1.107*	1.106*
	(0.020)		(0.020)	(0.049)	(0.048)
Year	0.962		0.965	0.959	0.962
	(0.022)		(0.022)	(0.045)	(0.047)
State associations					
Bavaria		1.395**	1.373*	1.030	1.019
		(0.179)	(0.176)	(0.164)	(0.162)
Brandenburg		0.930	0.810	2.306**	2.073*
		(0.128)	(0.120)	(0.724)	(0.695)
Hesse		1.241	1.254	0.698*	0.700*
		(0.169)	(0.171)	(0.116)	(0.117)
Mecklenburg-West Pomerania		0.567**	0.514***	0.715	0.926
		(0.101)	(0.096)	(0.279)	(0.351)
Middle Rhine		1.175	1.214	0.985	1.005
		(0.173)	(0.178)	(0.164)	(0.167)
Lower Saxony		1.345*	1.357*	1.134	1.139
		(0.178)	(0.179)	(0.183)	(0.184)
Rhineland		0.188***	0.186***	0.194***	0.195***
		(0.076)	(0.076)	(0.079)	(0.079)

(continued)

Table 2.2 (Cont.)

Independent variables	Adult teams per municipality				Youth teams per municipality			
	Model 1	Model 2	Model 3	Model 4	Model 5	Model 6	Model 7	Model 8
Saarland			1.800**	1.850**			0.755	0.762
			(0.330)	(0.339)			(0.171)	(0.173)
Schleswig-Holstein			1.958***	1.936***			1.481*	1.470*
			(0.281)	(0.278)			(0.271)	(0.269)
South Baden			1.945***	1.940***			1.346	1.346
			(0.277)	(0.275)			(0.232)	(0.232)
South West			0.201***	0.198***			0.158***	0.158***
			(0.055)	(0.054)			(0.047)	(0.047)

Note: *** $p < 0.001$; ** $p < 0.01$; * $p < 0.05$. East = Dummy variable for East German federal states; lnInhabitants = Natural logarithm of municipality inhabitants; County status = Dummy variable for municipalities enjoying county status; Women share = Women's share of municipality inhabitants; Youth share = Share of municipality inhabitants younger than 18 years; Social share = Share of inhabitants with an occupation subject to social insurance; Relative change = Relative population change. N = 37,893 observations and 9,474 groups, average number of observations per group is 4.0. Method is negative binomial panel regression. Displayed are incident rate ratios (IRRs).

Girls' and women's grass-roots soccer 39

team numbers. Hence, the analyses suggest that unfavorable macro-social conditions and institutional legacies in East Germany matter but they do not suffice to explain the geography of girls' and women's soccer in West Germany. Accordingly, the results can be interpreted as indicating that association policies significantly affect the development of girls' and women's soccer.

Moreover, although the multivariate statistics support the conclusion from the descriptive analyses that team numbers are significantly declining, the East–West gap does not widen. However, basic theoretical ideas are supported, insofar as girls' and women's soccer appears to be rather an urban phenomenon. The higher the number of inhabitants in a municipality, the higher the number of girls' and women's teams. Surprisingly and hard to explain is that the county status of a municipality serves to decrease the number of teams. Another interesting and counter-intuitive finding is that the number of adult teams decreases with a higher share of female inhabitants. However, in order to put this finding into perspective, it is important to note that the female inhabitant share is higher in more urban municipalities. The fact that a higher youth share corresponds with a higher number of youth teams is consistent with the theoretical reasoning on the importance of niche width. Moreover, girls' and women's soccer teams appear to be more present in municipalities with a better employment structure, that is, the number of teams increases with a higher share of people enjoying social insurance. Interestingly, general population trends do not leave a significant impact on team numbers.

The analyses of team survival report Hazard ratios, that is, the risk for team dissolution (Tables 2.3 and 2.4). A Hazard ratio greater than one indicates that a team of a specific category faces a higher risk of dissolution. Accordingly, a Hazard ratio of less than one indicates a lower risk. The analyses conducted for a ten-year period, which use the *County* status of municipalities as a proxy for urbanity, support the idea that team survival is more critical in East Germany. However, the models including the state association dummies indicate again substantial regional diversity (see Table 2.3, Models 9, 10, and 12). Thus, chances of team survival appear to be significantly higher in the West German state associations of Bavaria, Hesse, South Baden, and South West Germany but significantly lower in the West German state association of Saarland. However, urbanity as measured by the county status of a municipality does not significantly affect survival chances.

Furthermore, the findings indicate that belonging to lower leagues significantly increases the risks of team dissolution. Surprisingly, recent promotion *and* relegation serve to reduce the risks of team dissolution

Table 2.3 Analyzing team survival from seasons 2005/2006 to 2015/2016

Independent variables	Model 9	Model 10	Model 11	Model 12
East	1.236***	1.277***	1.150	1.203*
	(0.059)	(0.058)	(0.086)	(0.094)
County status	0.937	0.741	0.965	0.752
	(0.037)	(0.125)	(0.034)	(0.122)
East × County status		1.276		1.297
		(0.222)		(0.216)
League	1.037***	1.037***	1.103***	1.103***
	(0.006)	(0.006)	(0.009)	(0.009)
Promotion	0.784***	0.784***	0.833***	0.833***
	(0.022)	(0.022)	(0.023)	(0.023)
Relegation	0.957*	0.957*	0.952**	0.952**
	(0.018)	(0.018)	(0.018)	(0.018)
Age class				
A Juniors	4.667***	4.673***	5.334***	5.342***
	(0.184)	(0.185	(0.234)	(0.234)
B Juniors	2.473***	2.476***	2.617***	2.622***
	(0.053)	(0.053)	(0.057)	(0.057)
C Juniors	3.047***	3.051***	3.376***	3.382***
	(0.076)	(0.076)	(0.088)	(0.088)
D Juniors	2.776***	2.779***	3.167***	3.171***
	(0.076)	(0.076)	(0.092)	(0.092)
E Juniors	2.863***	2.866***	3.306***	3.310***
	(0.105)	(0.105)	(0.122)	(0.123)
F Juniors	3.737***	3.743***	4.337***	4.344***
	(0.369)	(0.369)	(0.431)	(0.432)
G Juniors				
Teams per club	0.958****	0.958***	0.952***	0.952***
	(0.004)	(0.004)	(0.004)	(0.004)
State associations				
Bavaria			0.699***	0.699***
			(0.031)	(0.031)
Brandenburg			0.954	0.939
			(0.095)	(0.091)
Middle Rhine			0.928	0.929
			(0.045)	(0.045)
Rhineland			1.084	1.086
			(0.058)	(0.058)
Hesse			0.765***	0.766***
			(0.040)	(0.040)
Mecklenburg-West Pomerania			1.115	1.101
			(0.114)	(0.111)
Lower Saxony			0.927	0.928
			(0.037)	(0.037)
Saarland			1.172	1.175**
			(0.061)	(0.061)

Girls' and women's grass-roots soccer 41

Table 2.3 (Cont.)

Independent variables	Model 9	Model 10	Model 11	Model 12
Schleswig-Holstein			1.049	1.050
			(0.047)	(0.046)
South Baden			0.757***	0.759***
			(0.037)	(0.037)
South West			0.886*	0.886*
			(0.048)	(0.048)

Notes: *** $p < 0.001$; ** $p < 0.01$; * $p < 0.05$. East = Dummy variable for East German federal states; County status = Dummy variable for municipalities enjoying county status; League = League to which the team belonged; Promotion = Dummy variable for a recently promoted team; Relegation = Dummy variable for a recently relegated team. Number of subjects= 19,259; number of failures = 15,011; times at risk = 58,750. Cox-Hazard-regressions, Breslow method for ties, standard errors adjusted for municipalities. a. Displayed are Hazard ratios and standard errors (in brackets). b. Reference category are ordinary municipalities. c. Reference category are adult teams. d. Reference category is Baden association. e. Not estimated due to low case numbers.

in the long-term dataset. Moreover, the multivariate analyses support the impression from the descriptive analyses that girls' soccer is facing higher risks of team dissolution. Hence, A Junior teams as well as F Junior teams face a particularly difficult time, just to survive. Moreover, teams from clubs investing more effort into girls' and women's soccer, as measured by *Teams per club*, face much greater chances of survival.

The short-term survival analyses, which cover only a four-year period but include more sophisticated context indicators, do not fully support these findings (Table 2.4). A simple model indicates again higher risks of East German teams to dissolve (Model 13). However, introducing interaction effects as well as association dummies serves to reverse the *East* effect and to render it insignificant (Models 14, 15, and 16). Again, the East German state associations Brandenburg, Mecklenburg-West Pomerania, and Thuringia seem to be characterized by higher risks of team dissolution. Yet, these effects are statistically not significant. In contrast, teams belonging to the two West German state associations Bavaria and Hesse are significantly more likely to survive.

Furthermore, the analyses provide support for the idea that contextual factors, such as a better employment structure and a more favorable population balance, improve the survival chances of women's soccer teams. Surprisingly, and in contradiction to the theoretical reasoning, a better employment structure as well as a more favorable population balance serve to increase the risks of team dissolution in East Germany. Again, belonging to a lower league increases risks of

Table 2.4 Girls' and women's soccer team survival from seasons 2011/2012 to 2015/2016

	Model 13	Model 14	Model 15	Model 16
East	1.415***	0.080	0.953	0.056
	(0.111)	(0.331)	(0.356)	(0.236)
lnInhabitants	0.978	0.982	0.981	0.986
	(0.012)	(0.012)	(0.013)	(0.013)
Women share	1.021	1.022	1.019	1.020
	(0.019)	(0.020)	(0.019)	(0.020)
Youth share	1.015	1.020	1.015	1.021
	(0.012)	(0.013)	(0.013)	(0.013)
Social share	0.959***	0.957***	0.967***	0.965***
	(0.005)	(0.005)	(0.005)	(0.006)
Relative change	0.860***	0.851***	0.858***	0.849***
	(0.012)	(0.013)	(0.013)	(0.013)
East ×				
lnInhabitants		0.947		0.943
		(0.054)		(0.055)
Women share		1.044		1.052
		(0.080)		(0.082)
Youth share		0.942		0.935
		(0.050)		(0.051)
Social share		1.054**		1.046*
		(0.021)		(0.021)
Relative change		1.153**		1.158**
		(0.054)		(0.055)
League	1.036*	1.037*	1.099***	1.097***
	(0.016)	(0.016)	(0.021)	(0.021)
Promotion	0.826***	0.826***	0.887*	0.882*
	(0.044)	(0.044)	(0.049)	(0.049)
Relegation	1.092*	1.089*	1.085*	1.082
	(0.045)	(0.045)	(0.045)	(0.045)
Age class				
A Juniors	4.256***	4.269***	4.910***	4.904***
	(0.414)	(0.414)	(0.506)	(0.503)
B Juniors	2.612***	2.626***	2.778***	2.782***
	(0.126)	(0.127)	(0.136)	(0.137)
C Juniors	3.035***	3.054***	3.426***	3.426***
	(0.174)	(0.175)	(0.211)	(0.210)
D Juniors	2.809***	2.825***	3.236***	3.229***
	(0.178)	(0.179)	(0.224)	(0.223)
E Juniors	2.954***	2.967***	3.455***	3.443***
	(0.237)	(0.239)	(0.309)	(0.308)
F Juniors	5.982***	5.993***	6.762***	6.733***
	1.206)	(1.211)	(1.389)	(1.385)
G Juniors				
Teams per club	0.867***	0.867***	0.867***	0.867***
	(0.011)	(0.011)	(0.011)	(0.011)

Girls' and women's grass-roots soccer   43

Table 2.4 (Cont.)

	Model 13	Model 14	Model 15	Model 16
State associations				
Bavaria			0.723***	0.730***
			(0.058)	(0.058)
Brandenburg			1.377	1.403
			(0.542)	(0.532)
Middle Rhine			0.866	0.855
			(0.070)	(0.069)
Rhineland			1.034	1.023
			(0.262)	(0.261)
Hesse			0.837*	0.836*
			(0.074)	(0.074)
Mecklenburg-West Pomerania			1.391	1.402
			(0.568)	(0.561)
Lower Saxony			0.927	0.922
			(0.067)	(0.067)
Saarland			1.102	1.103
			(0.127)	(0.129)
Schleswig-Holstein			1.118	1.115
			(0.104)	(0.104)
South Baden			0.871	0.868
			(0.087)	(0.087)
South West			1.054	1.047
			(0.156)	(0.153)
Thuringia			1.391	1.277
			(0.545)	(0.491)

Notes: *** $p < 0.001$; ** $p < 0.01$; * $p < 0.05$. East = Dummy variable for East German federal states; lnInhabitants = Natural logarithm of municipality inhabitants; County status = Dummy variable for municipalities enjoying county status; Women share = Women's share of municipality inhabitants; Youth share = Share of municipality inhabitants younger than 18 years; Social share = Share of inhabitants with an occupation subject to social insurance; Relative change = Relative population change; League = League to which the team belonged; Promotion = Dummy variable for a recently promoted team; Relegation = Dummy variable for a recently relegated team. Number of subjects = 6,835; number of failures = 3,176; times at risk = 16,481. Cox-Hazard-regressions, Breslow method for ties, standard errors adjusted for municipalities. a. Displayed are Hazard ratios and standard errors (in brackets). b. Reference category are ordinary municipalities. c. Reference category are adult teams. d. Reference category is Baden association. e. Not estimated due to low case numbers.

team dissolution. Recent promotion serves to reduce these risks while, in more recent periods, relegation seems to make team dissolution more likely. Moreover, the models support the conclusion that girls' teams face higher risks of dissolution. Hence, A Junior teams as well as F Junior teams seem to have a particularly hard time just to survive. Finally, teams from clubs more committed to girls' and women's soccer, as measured by *Teams per club*, enjoy greater chances of survival.

Conclusion

This chapter has been dedicated to the development of grass-roots girls' and women's soccer in Germany. The analyses of a unique dataset on competitive teams yielded some important theoretical and practical insights. First, although there has been a substantial increase in the number of girls' and women's soccer teams, the more recent developments serve to question the idea that the future of soccer will be (more) female. Team numbers are stagnating and substantial problems in maintaining youth teams have become evident.

With regard to Germany's character as a natural experiment for examining the impact of macro-social trends and policy legacies on the development of girls' and women's soccer, the analyses brought about complex findings. As has been argued, East Germany is characterized by both, unfavorable macro-social conditions and problematic institutional legacies, which should result in a persistent and even increasing East–West gap in the development of girls' and women's soccer. Economic decline and out-migration should serve to further marginalize girls' and women's soccer in East Germany because communist sports policies were likely to derogate resource claims of girls' and women's soccer. The analyses provided some support for these ideas as, in East Germany, team numbers are in general lower and girls' and women's soccer teams face higher chances of dissolution. However, contrary to the theoretical expectations, the East–West gap does not widen—yet also does not close. In general, the analyses support the idea that macro-social factors and institutional legacies are relevant for understanding the geography of girls' and women's soccer. However, it also becomes evident that macro-social factors and institutional legacies are not sufficient to account for the regional diversity found in West Germany. Some West German state associations are substantially 'underperforming' even in comparison to East German state associations. These findings are of utmost theoretical and practical importance.

On a theoretical level, the analyses support efforts to understand sport as spatially constrained activity and to explore the impact of variations in macro-social factors on the spatial distribution of sports. Thus, the analyses confirm previous insights according to which the maintenance of competitive sport becomes increasingly difficult in rural municipalities and/or municipalities facing economic problems and outmigration. Nevertheless, the analyses indicate that for understanding the spatial organization of girls' and women's soccer, it does not suffice to focus on macro-social factors but that meso-level factors need to be taken into account. In other words, it would be wrong to adopt a deterministic perspective on the impact of macro-social conditions. The significant differences between state associations, when it comes to team numbers, nurture the interpretation that policies adopted at the association level might play a decisive role for the development of girls' and women's soccer. By implication, the legacies of East German sports policies appear to be less decisive and less persistent as theoretically assumed. Moreover, notwithstanding the relevance of macro-social factors, the state associations enjoy some discretion in promoting the development of girls' and women's soccer, even under unfavorable conditions. Thus, although the analyses indicate substantial growth problems in younger cohorts, they do not allow for the conclusion that the potential for girls' and women's soccer in Germany has been exhausted. The substantial gap between the leading state association of Lower Saxony and most other state associations suggests that there is still growth potential. Lower Saxony might serve as a benchmark for other German state associations because the federal state is characterized by substantial socio-demographic and economic diversity and covers a huge territory. Thus, in theoretical terms, understanding the geography of girls' and women's soccer needs to take institutional and organizational factors in more detail into account, as was possible here.

In practical terms, the analyses support the idea that macro-social conditions influence the prospects of girls' and women's soccer. The analyses provide some support for the idea that, due to a shrinking target population and more intense resource competition in rural areas, girls' and women's soccer is more likely to represent an urban phenomenon. More urban municipalities are more likely to host a higher number of girls' and women's teams. In contrast, the evidence for an impact of urbanity on team survival is substantially weaker. Yet, it seems that better employment structures and demographic viability of municipalities affect team survival. Thus, in accordance with the theoretical ideas, it can be concluded that local contexts are relevant for the development of girls' and women's soccer. However, the analyses fail to provide clues as to how associations and clubs manage to promote and maintain girls' and womens' soccer, even under unfavorable conditions. Thus, in practical terms, more detailed case studies on best practice at association and club levels are needed. Hence, the most successful girls' and women's soccer clubs in different socio-demographic and economic contexts should be examined in order to identify crucial success factors at the club level. The importance of meso-level factors is indicated by the fact that the number of girls' and women's soccer teams that a club

46 *Girls' and women's grass-roots soccer*

organizes serves to increase the chances of team survival. The finding comes with substantial policy implications. It suggests that clubs need to make a serious commitment to girls' and women's soccer if such efforts are to be sustainable. Hence, the findings support the, not surprising, conclusion that lukewarm initiatives to create isolated girls' or women's teams within a club are not likely to create an environment in which girls' and women's soccer can prosper.

3 Stadium attendance in women's league soccer

Introduction

In 1987, the West German DFB decided to create a full-fledged national league for women's soccer from the 1990/1991 season on, which coincided with German reunification. Before this, the soccer association in both Germanys had experimented with different forms of national competitions for women's soccer.

The first West German national championships, which were organized from 1974 onwards, represented knock-out competitions between regional champions. However, from the 1985/1986 season, the West German DFB decided to create regional league competitions. As these regional leagues proved to be highly imbalanced, the DFB finally opted for creating a national women's league in 1990. In contrast, women's soccer remained not only permanently under-resourced in East Germany, but also the East German soccer association simply refused to establish a full national league due to concerns about escalating traveling costs. Accordingly, the national women's soccer competition was denied the title of a national championship (see Chapter 1). To make matters worse, the East German soccer association repeatedly tinkered with the design of the competition (Hennies & Meuren, 2011: 180). Only from the season 1987/1988, was a two-tier national league created (Hoffmann & Nendza, 2006: 144). As a result, East Germany was not only characterized by an underdeveloped grass-roots movement of girls' and women's soccer, but also by a lack of professional structures among the clubs competing at the national level, which resulted in a substantial lag in athletic performances.

Reunified Germany's first national women's soccer league, introduced in 1990, represented a two-tier competition with a North and South division. This particular competitive structure was chosen due to concerns about athletic quality and traveling costs. However, team

48 *Stadium attendance in women's soccer*

quality continued to differ substantially, which resulted in very uneven competitions. In order to increase athletic quality as well as competitive balance, the DFB decided to create a one-tier league called Frauen-Bundesliga (FBL) in 1997/1998, consisting of 12 teams. The DFB had high expectations concerning stadium attendance, media attention, and professionalization. These expectations did not fully materialize (Hoffmann & Nendza, 2006: 150–151) so that some observers even characterized the FBL as the 'problem child' of German women's soccer (Hennies & Meuren, 2011: 165). Hence, in contrast to the national team, the FBL hardly receives any media attention (Küchenmeister & Schneider, 2014), and the league's limited commercial success is also indicated by the fact that the players are still only semi-professional (Tagesspiegel, 2017). However, there is no doubt that, in athletic terms, the FBL provides its fans with a top-quality soccer experience. FBL teams have won club competitions organized by UEFA nine times since their introduction in the 2001/2002 season.[1] The German women's national soccer team, which is primarily composed of FBL players, has until recently almost constantly delivered top performances (see Chapter 5). Yet, the creation of the FBL did not serve to mitigate the persistent competitive imbalance within German women's soccer. Of the 33 teams playing in the league in the period from 2001 to 2002, only five won the championship.[2] Two commonly used measures for the uncertainty of league outcomes—that is, the standard deviation of points gained by each team by the end of the season and the correlation of team rankings between two subsequent seasons—suggest not only that competitive imbalance is high but also even increasing (Figure 3.1). A previous study on league attendance in the FBL concluded that the top teams monopolize national playing talent and solidify their dominant status (Meier et al., 2016).

Furthermore, it should be noted that the semi-professional FBL appears to represent a difficult environment for women's soccer teams. The FBL has seen a substantial turnover in terms of team composition. More than 40 percent of all teams promoted to the FBL have been immediately relegated and less than one-fifth of the teams has survived more than 11 seasons (Figure 3.2). However, a common trend in the period after 2009 has been that 'big' men's clubs have started fielding women's teams. These teams usually enjoy higher budgets and have succeeded in displacing former pioneers of women's soccer. Hence, the FFC Heike Rheine, the first independent German soccer club, was dissolved in 2016 after the drain of the most talented players to more metropolitan clubs had resulted in a long-lasting sporting crisis. The displacement of pioneer women's soccer clubs seems to reflect a more

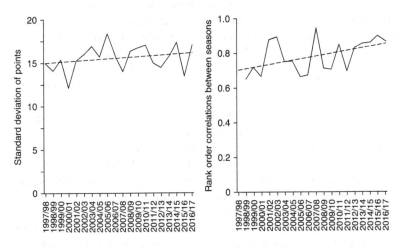

Figure 3.1 Competitive balance in the Frauen-Bundesliga

Notes: Left-hand figure displays standard deviation of points scored by the FBL teams at the end of the season and the linear trend. Right-hand figure displays correlation between the rankings of the FBL teams in two consecutive seasons. Dashed lines represent linear trends.

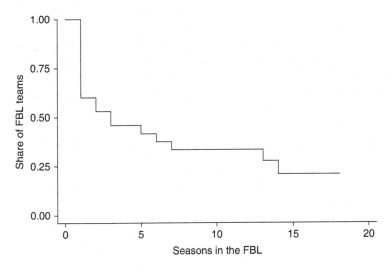

Figure 3.2 Team survival in the Frauen-Bundesliga

general trend in European women's soccer (Klein, 2018). The case of the English women's soccer club Doncaster Belles illustrates that the rationale to professionalize and to commercialize women's soccer works against pioneer clubs. The Belles were one of the most famous clubs in English women's soccer with a 22-year tradition of playing in the top division. However, the English soccer association (the FA) decided in 2013 that the Belles—although qualified on sporting merits—would not be part of a reorganized Women's Super League in 2014. The FA based its decision on four criteria: financial management, commercial sustainability, facilities, and player and youth development. The place of the Belles was given to Manchester City. Although Manchester City had fielded a women's team in national women's competition for only one season and did not qualify for promotion, the club—owned by one of the richest people in world—could score in terms of commercial and financial sustainability (Rich, 2013; Williamson, 2013). In Germany, the mechanisms of displacement work slightly differently but have the same effect. It seems that some major men's clubs have intensified their efforts due to the perception that a major soccer club by now needs to have a strong women's division (e.g., Eder, 2018). In the case of Bayern Munich, its former President Franz Beckenbauer was so impressed by the performances at the 1999 Women's World Cup that he quadrupled the budget for the club's women's division. Other major clubs, such as Bayer 04 Leverkusen, TSG 1899 Hoffenheim, and VfL Wolfsburg took over women's teams or clubs facing financial difficulties or organizational limitations. In the case of VfL Wolfsburg, the move was supported by the club's main sponsor, Volkswagen, which expected a substantial promotional impact from supporting a women's soccer team (Meuren, 2015). By heavily subsidizing women's soccer teams, the major clubs have literally changed the playing field in German women's soccer. Even though the budgets for women's soccer pale in comparison to the budgets for the men's squads, the presence of major clubs has served to raise the bar for all women's soccer teams in terms of facilities, coaching, and player salaries. Increased European competition exerts similar effects (Klein, 2018). Smaller pioneer women's soccer clubs, in particular those located in provincial regions, are inevitably outcompeted.

In accordance with the 'future of soccer is feminine' *leitmotif* of this book, this chapter is set out to study the development of stadium attendance in the FBL. More precisely, it will first ask whether there is a growth in stadium attendance over time. Previous research found substantial evidence that the league attracted mainly 'diehard' fans who did not care much about the attractiveness of the competition

Stadium attendance in women's soccer 51

(Meier, Konjer, & Leinwather, 2016). Therefore, the second question to be addressed here is whether women's soccer still represents a niche product primarily consumed by a highly dedicated core audience. In order to address these questions, theoretical and methodological standard approaches derived from sports economics will be employed. Accordingly, the discussion will first explore which factors usually drive stadium attendance.

Determinants of stadium attendance

As the analysis of stadium attendance represents one of the key pillars of empirical sports economics, there exists an impressive stock of empirical research (for excellent reviews see Borland & MacDonald, 2003; Szymanski, 2003; Buraimo, 2006; Feehan, 2006; Simmons, 2006; García & Rodríguez, 2009). Research on stadium attendance has covered a quite diverse range of sports from different countries. Therefore, the following review of research findings will put particular emphasis on findings on stadium attendance in German men's soccer.

First of all, research has established that stadium visitors are loyal consumers whose demand is characterized by considerable 'habit persistence' (e.g., Borland & Lye, 1992; Feehan, 2006; Ferreira & Bravo, 2007; Buraimo, 2008). These findings hold true for German soccer attendance as well as those suggested by the studies of Frick et al. (1999), Czarnitzki and Stadtmann (2002), and Pawlowski and Anders (2012). Notwithstanding habitual persistence, stadium attendance is influenced by host site characteristics, economic factors, and product characteristics specific to team sports (Borland & MacDonald, 2003).

Concerning the impact of host site-related characteristics on stadium attendance, scholars have found that population size and regional income matter (Simmons, 1996; Downward & Dawson, 2000; Feehan, 2006; Ferreira & Bravo, 2007). The impact of local income on attendance has, however, remained ambiguous. There is some evidence that demand decreases with higher local income, suggesting that team sports represent an inferior good (Bird, 1982; Jones & Ferguson, 1988; Cairns, 1990; Borland & Lye, 1992). However, more recent research suggests that at least top division soccer represents a normal (Baimbridge et al., 1996) or even a luxury good (Simmons, 1996). Inconsistent results have also been presented concerning the impact of unemployment rates on attendance. Whereas Dobson and Goddard (1996) found that unemployment decreased attendance, Borland and Macdonald (2003: 481) have argued that (certain) sports events might 'constitute a social outlet for unemployed persons'.

52 *Stadium attendance in women's soccer*

With regard to the relevance of site-related factors for soccer attendance in Germany, there is evidence that attendance is increased by the size of the home market (Czarnitzki & Stadtmann, 2002) and regional average income (Gärtner & Pommerehne, 1978; Feddersen et al., 2006; Feddersen & Maennig, 2007). Moreover, improvements in stadium quality seem to leave a positive and lasting effect on stadium attendance, with consumers preferring single-purpose facilities (Feddersen et al., 2006; Feddersen & Maennig, 2007; Rottmann & Seitz, 2008). Concerning local competition, Breuer (2009) found, surprisingly, that rivalry between two top division clubs in a city seemed to increase aggregate stadium attendance. Unfortunately, none of the studies on German soccer controlled for regional unemployment rates.

With respect to the costs of stadium attendance, there is consensus that demand is price inelastic in the short run (Simmons, 1996; Carmichael et al., 1999; Downward & Dawson, 2000; Fort, 2004), with occasional spectators being more price sensitive (Welki & Zlatoper, 1994; Simmons, 1996). However, it has been proposed to not just consider ticket prices but the total costs of stadium attendance (Ferreira & Bravo, 2007). Accordingly, traveling costs seem to leave a negative effect on demand (see Borland & MacDonald, 2003). Furthermore, opportunity costs and weather conditions matter for stadium attendance (cf. Buraimo, 2008). Unfortunately, studies on stadium attendance in German soccer have so far rarely considered price or cost variables. The early study conducted by Gärtner and Pommerehne (1978) found that attendance decreased with higher prices. However, the authors suggested a cautious interpretation due to the unreliability of their price data. Czarnitzki and Stadtmann (2002) included the distance between home and away teams, which could serve as a proxy for traveling and opportunity costs, in their analyses but found no significant effect. Furthermore, the evidence on the impact of weather conditions has remained inconsistent. Czarnitzki and Stadtmann (2002) found no evidence for a weather-related attendance effect while Rottmann and Seitz (2008) detected a significant positive impact of temperature, and Gärtner and Pommerehne (1978) and Pawlowski and Anders (2012) a negative impact of precipitation.

Regarding product characteristics specific to sporting competitions, it is incontrovertible that team success increases attendance (Welki & Zlatoper, 1994; Ferreira & Bravo, 2007; Buraimo, 2008). Furthermore, the sporting quality of the involved teams is relevant for stadium attendance (Dobson & Goddard, 1996; Kuypers, 1996; García & Rodríguez, 2002) as well as the presence of superstar players (Berri et al., 2004). The importance of sporting quality for soccer attendance in Germany has

Stadium attendance in women's soccer 53

been proved ever since the very first studies were conducted. Melzer and Stäglin (1965) showed that the concentration of sporting quality, by the creation of a one-tier top division, heavily reduced attendance for lower divisions. Moreover, early work demonstrated that better rankings of the involved teams increased match attendance (Melzer & Stäglin, 1965; Gärtner & Pommerehne, 1978; Büch, 1979). Furthermore, as Gärtner and Pommerehne (1978) and Czarnitzki and Stadtmann (2002) showed, a team's long-term sporting reputation has a positive effect on stadium attendance in German men's soccer. Rottmann and Seitz (2008), as well as Brandes and Franck (2007), arrived at similar conclusions, and Pawlowski and Anders (2012) also found a strong brand effect of the away team on stadium attendance. Finally, Brandes et al. (2008) found evidence for star effects in German top division soccer. Accordingly, soccer superstars enhanced attendance both at home and on the road, whereas local heroes enhanced only home attendance.

The uncertainty of the outcome hypothesis (UOH), that is, which sport consumers prefer, more uncertain competitions represent a founding pillar in the economics of sport (Rottenberg, 1956; Neale, 1964). Accordingly, UOH has attracted substantial scholarly attention. However, it is fair to conclude that the empirical findings have remained inconclusive so far (Szymanski, 2003; Pawlowski, 2013). There are several reasons for these inconsistent findings: First, UOH is not rooted in a sophisticated model of consumer behavior (Coates et al., 2014). Second, as Pawlowski (2013) has stressed, the common method for examining UOH—by relying on revealed preferences, that is, correlations between uncertainty measures and business success indicators—does not pay enough attention to fan perceptions. Third, the debate is complicated by the use of diverse metrics referring to the different time horizons of uncertainty, such as match outcome uncertainty, uncertainty about league or seasonal outcomes and the long-term dominance of particular teams (e.g., Feehan, 2006; Brandes & Franck, 2007; Lee & Fort, 2008; García & Rodríguez, 2009).

Regarding match outcome uncertainty, scholars seem to agree that uncertainty over match outcomes matters. Yet, contrary to the assumption of classic contributions on UOH (Rottenberg, 1956; Neale, 1964), maximum uncertainty does not maximize attendance. Some findings suggest that stadium attendance is highest when the home team enjoys an advantage but the match is not too one-sided (e.g., Knowles et al., 1992; Peel & Thomas, 1992; Forrest & Simmons, 2002). Thus, the relationship between uncertainty and demand seemed to resemble an inverted U (see Feehan, 2006; Simmons, 2006; see also Szymanski, 2003: 1156). More recent evidence from European first division soccer,

54   *Stadium attendance in women's soccer*

presented by Buraimo and Simmons (2008, 2009), suggests, however, that the relationship between match outcome uncertainty and attendance resembles a standard U form. An increase in match outcome uncertainty appeared to be associated with reduced demand. Fans seemed to prefer to see their team either play a much more inferior team, or to assume an outsider role in a 'David vs. Goliath' constellation, than to attend a game that is predicted to be close in score.

For Germany, the findings on UOH are likewise complex. Whereas Büch (1979) suggested that decreasing long-term uncertainty served to lower match attendance, more recent works arrived at different findings concerning the relevance of long-term uncertainty. Frick et al. (1999) suggested a negative effect of decreasing long-term uncertainty on attendance but stressed that the effect was rather small because the decrease in ticket demand for less successful teams was almost completely compensated by higher ticket demand for more successful teams. More recently, Brandes and Franck (2007: 389) found that 'the data from the 1. Bundesliga do not provide a basis for organizational regulations or restrictions aimed at maintaining competitive balance in order to secure fan attendance'. Pawlowski et al. (2010) also pointed to the fact that season aggregate attendance in the men's Bundesliga had increased, even though the league had become more dominated by a small number of teams.

Concerning the relevance of short- or medium-term uncertainty in German men's soccer, the findings have remained contradictory. Gärtner and Pommerehne (1978) found no evidence for short-term uncertainty but instead support for the relevance of medium-term uncertainty. Czarnitzki and Stadtmann (2002) could not detect any impact from short-term or medium-term uncertainty. In contrast, Rottmann and Seitz (2008) suggested a significant effect of short-term and medium-term uncertainty. Using quantile regressions in order to account for heterogeneity in fan demand, Benz et al. (2009) concluded that short-term uncertainty represents only a 'second-order' influence factor for attendance demand with a team's reputation being much more important. Moreover, match outcome uncertainty was found to affect high-demand matches only. The most recent evidence presented by Pawlowski and Anders (2012) detects a positive impact of medium-term uncertainty but a negative effect of short-term uncertainty.

In summary, empirical results on determinants of match attendance in German men's soccer are in line with more general findings of empirical sports economics. The demand for stadium attendance shows patterns of habit persistence and is influenced by host site characteristics as well as by economic factors and quality features specific to sport.

Team reputation and star presence play an important role in demand. Even the inconsistent German findings on UOH reflect the state of the art in empirical sports economics. However, until now it is open to debate to what extent these findings apply to women's soccer. The few survey-based marketing studies comparing consumer satisfaction for women's and men's games found evidence for a (slightly) higher relevance of venue-related factors and product extension quality (e.g., Trail et al. 2002), as well as for ticket prices and social aspects of the match experience for women's games (Fink et al., 2002). However, a previous investigation of FBL attendance found that the main predictor of demand was habit persistence; more precisely, it seemed that FBL matches were primarily attended by 'diehard' fans and that quality features played only a secondary role and venue-related factors almost none at all (Meier, Konjer, & Nagm, 2017). Thus, besides tracing the development of attendance data for more recent periods, this chapter will ask whether the characterization of the FBL as a niche product, consumed by a dedicated core audience, still holds true. If the latter is the case, attendance in the women's league soccer should continue to be determined by loyalty or habit persistence. In contrast, venue features, athletic quality, outcome uncertainty, and opportunity costs should be less relevant.

Analyzing attendance data in first-tier women's league soccer

Official attendance data for the one-tier FBL have been available since the 1998/1999 season (DFB, 2018). The empirical approach adopted here follows very much the conventions of the econometric analyses of stadium attendance (see Borland & Lye, 1992; Pawlowski & Anders, 2012). Hence, attendance for the home team serves as the dependent variable ($Attendance_t$). In order to account for consumer loyalty or habit persistence, lagged measures for short-term attendance ($Attendance_{t-1}$; $AttendanceAwayMatch_{t-1}$) as well as inter-seasonal attendance were included ($MeanAttHome_{Season-1}$; $MeanAttAway_{Season-1}$). There exists a significant positive trend toward higher average home team attendance ($r = 0.562$; $p < 0.001$) as well as higher average away team attendance ($r = 0.747$; $p < 0.001$), which means that for teams that manage to survive in the FBL, the consumer base seems to be increasing.

The sporting quality of the FBL matches was measured by the league positions of the two involved teams ($HomeRank$ and $AwayRank$). In order to account for the role of uncertainty, the measure for championship uncertainty (UCS) developed by Janssens and Késenne (1987) was used. Match outcome uncertainty was considered by two dummy

56 *Stadium attendance in women's soccer*

variables, which were calculated based on the rankings of the two teams in a fixture. *David* refers to constellations where the home team competes against a much better ranked away team (*Difference* ≥ 5) and *Goliath* indicates constellations where the home team appears to be superior to the away team (*Difference* ≤ –5).

A number of indicators serve to account for the home team's site characteristics. First, it was taken into account that some women's teams have changed their club affiliation in order to adapt to the organizational challenges of first-tier league soccer. These changes in club affiliations were motivated by two quite different considerations: Some women's soccer teams decided to walk out of men dominated clubs, which was particularly characteristic for the beginning of women's soccer in West Germany (Hoffmann & Nendza, 2006: 167). Such secessions can be reasonable since women's teams no longer have to compete with the much longer-established men's teams over scarce club resources. Moreover, independent women's teams might enjoy better access to training facilities provided by the municipalities. However, other women's teams have switched clubs for economic concerns, such as insolvency, or hope for better commercial prospects by joining a 'big' men's soccer club (Table 3.1). In the case of Wolfsburg, a successful women's soccer team existed there for quite some time. When the original club VfR Eintracht Wolfsburg became insolvent, the team became affiliated to the rather provincial club WSB Wendschott 1996. In 2003, the team switched to VfL Wolfsburg in order to benefit from the marketing power of the club, which originated from several company sport clubs of German automaker Volkswagen. The FFC Brauweiler

Table 3.1 Changes in team affiliations in the Frauen-Bundesliga

Year	Pre-transformation	Post-transformation	Nature of transformation
1998	FC Eintracht Rheine	FFC Heike Rheine	Creation of an independent women's club
1999	SG Praunheim	1. FFC Frankfurt	Creation of an independent women's club
2000	Grün-Weiß Brauweiler	FFC Brauweiler Pulheim 2000	Creation of an independent women's club
2001	FCR Duisburg 55	FCR 2001 Duisburg	Creation of an independent women's club
2003	WSV Wolfsburg-Wendschott	VfL Wolfsburg	Club switch due to better commercial prospects
2009	FFC Brauweiler Pulheim 2000	1. FC Köln	Club switch after insolvency

Source: DFB, teams' websites, author's own depiction.

Stadium attendance in women's soccer 57

Pulheim 2000 originally represented the result of a walkout of a successful women's soccer division from a men's dominated club. After the club had entered a typical downward spiral of athletic failure and decreasing revenues (in general, see Szymanski, 2014), it went bankrupt. In the aftermath, the entire club switched to 1. FC Köln, one of the biggest sports clubs in Germany and a soccer powerhouse. Hence, two dummy variables were coded: The first variable, *Independence*, refers to the 'secession' of women's teams from male-dominated clubs. The second variable, *Switch*, represents mergers of women's soccer teams with established men's clubs.

Concerning venue related factors, six dummy variables for stadium quality were coded:

- *Quality1*: small sports ground without terraces or spectator facilities
- *Quality2*: small multipurpose sports ground with some terrace constructions
- *Quality3*: smaller football stadium without seated terraces
- *Quality4*: smaller football stadium with seated terraces
- *Quality5*: multipurpose stadium with a crowd capacity of more than 3500
- *Quality6*: football stadium with a crowd capacity of more than 3500

This coding of stadium quality indicates that the diversity in stadium quality found among FBL clubs has been quite substantial. Moreover, it is hard to conceive that men's top division soccer would be played on sports grounds without any infrastructure for spectators. However, stadium quality has substantially improved over time as no league matches were played in stadiums of the lowest quality since the season 2008/2009. Furthermore, since the 2013/2014 season, more than 50 percent of all league matches were staged in facilities of the highest quality (Figure 3.3). These improvements in stadium quality result primarily from changes in FBL membership composition but not from stadium quality improvements at the team level. Only seven of the 33 FBL teams experienced such improvements, which did not appear to be motivated by long-term or short-term increases in stadium attendance (Meier, Konjer, & Leinwather, 2016).

The urbanity of the home team site was operationalized by regional population density in the county of the home team (*Density*). Still, the population density of host sites continues to differ substantially. In the 2016/2017 season, population density ranged from 88.2 inhabitants/km² (SC Sand—Ortenaukreis county) to 4,712.9 inhabitants/km² (*FC* Bayern München—Munich county). The analyses also include a regional income indicator, which suffers, however, from shortcomings of official

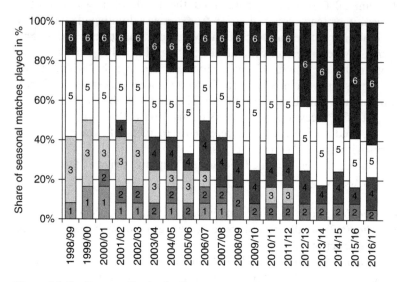

Figure 3.3 Stadium quality in the Frauen-Bundesliga

Notes: 1 = Small sports ground w/o spectator facilities; 2 = Small multipurpose sports ground, 3 = Smaller football stadium w/o seated terraces; 4 = Smaller football stadium with seated terraces; 5 = Multipurpose stadium (capacity > 3,500); 6 = Football stadium (capacity > 3,500).

German statistics (*Real income*). Historical records of ticket price data are not available for the FBL. While it can be reasonably assumed that for some time a number of sites did not charge visitors at all and indeed some continue to do so, by now at least the top teams demand that visitors pay, albeit at a very moderate level.[3] Given the lack of reliable data, no ticket price data indicator could be included. In order to account for traveling costs for away fans, a variable for the geographical distance between the home and the away team was created (*Distance*). Opportunity costs were operationalized with a dummy for matches staged on Saturdays and Sundays (*Weekend*). Since most matches in the FBL are played in the late morning, dummies for matches beginning in the afternoon (3 pm to 6.30 pm) (*Afternoon*) and for evening matches beginning later than 7 pm (*Evening*) were included. In addition, the weather conditions at the time of the kick-off were determined using data from the public archives of the German Meteorological Service (Deutscher Wetterdienst—DWD). The amount of rainfall was recoded according to common conventions (*Rain*), with the coding of the temperature data distinguished between four categories (*Temp*).

With regard to trends in FBL attendance, *Season* was coded as a set of distinct seasonal dummies. This procedure not only avoids multicollinearity problems but also allows for detecting non-linear trends and for tracing the impact of achievements of the national women's soccer team on FBL attendance. As discussed in the introductory chapter, the national women's soccer team has been the sport's most visible outlet in Germany (Hennies & Meuren, 2011: 135–140). Thus, at least in the case of the 2011 'home' World Cup, the DFB expected that the event would also serve to boost FBL attendance. While the event created unprecedented media attention for women's soccer in Germany, the DFB's apparently aggressive marketing campaign was likely to backfire on the sport (see Chapter 4). Since LeFeuvre et al. (2013) found that the dramatic performance of the USA team during the World Cup served to double attendance for league matches, it seemed likely that a successful performance of the women's national soccer team would have an effect on FBL attendance.

In the German case, effects might show for the 2003/2004 as well as for 2007/2008 seasons because the women's national team won the World Cup before these seasons. If the successful performance in the European Championships affected league attendance, those effects should materialize in the seasons of 2001/2002, 2005/2006, 2009/2010 and 2013/2014 since the national team won the European Championships before these seasons. The year 2016 might also show an effect as the national team won the Olympic soccer tournament in that year. In addition two dummy variables were coded in order to account for a short-term impact of national team success on league attendance (*AfterTitle3*; *AfterTitle6*).

The analytic strategy followed the suggestion of Forrest and Simmons (2006) to organize the dataset as a cross-sectional time series in which home teams serve as cross-sectional units and the match day as the time variable. As it has been assumed that women's soccer represents a niche product for diehard fans, the first models include only habit persistence indicators. In a next step, predictors accounting for host site characteristics and quality features of sports entertainment were included.

Stagnation at low levels

Depicting average attendance figures for the FBL over time reveals a substantial growth in average crowd size, which has almost quadrupled from 254 visitors in the 1998/1999 season to 946 in the 2016/2017 season. However, in comparison to average crowd sizes for men's soccer, these figures are still very low. In the 2016/2017 season, a first division men's match attracted on average 41,514 visitors; a second division match 21,717 visitors; and a third division match still 5,970 visitors. However, in comparison to other European women's leagues, the FBL does not perform particularly badly. In the 2016/2017 season, English women's first-tier soccer teams attracted on average 1,058 visitors and French teams around 708. All three leagues were characterized by stagnating or even declining average attendance figures (Magowan, 2019). Yet, European attendance figures pale in comparison to the US American National Women's Soccer League (NWSL), whose teams attracted, on average, 6,024 stadium visitors in the 2018 season.

Moreover, even though FBL attendance has substantially increased over the entire period, there is no continuous linear trend. Surprisingly, attendance experienced a boost in the post 'home' World Cup season of 2011/2012 even though the national team's performance was widely considered to be disappointing. In the subsequent season, average attendance dropped substantially, grew again in the following season and seems now to be slowly declining. In addition, seasons with higher average attendance appear to be characterized by increased variance in attendance among FBL teams (Figure 3.4).

The multivariate models presented in Table 3.2 confirm, first, that attendance has significantly grown in the period under scrutiny but that there is no linear trend after the 2011/2012 season. More precisely, FBL

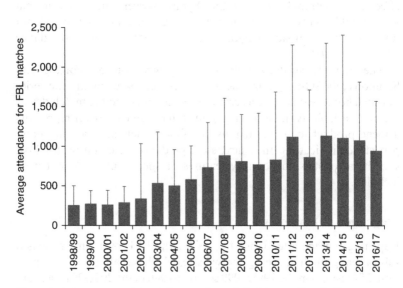

Figure 3.4 Average attendance for matches of the Frauen-Bundesliga

Table 3.2 Attendance for Frauen-Bundesliga matches

Independent variables	Model 1	Model 2	Model 3	Model 4
	Short-term habit persistence	*Medium-term habit persistence*	*Full model without medium-term habit persistence*	*Full model with medium-term habit persistence*
Habit persistence indicators				
ln Attendance$_{t-1}$	0.254***	0.222***	0.186***	0.179***
	(0.020)	(0.023)	(0.018)	(0.022)
ln AwayAttendance$_{t-1}$	0.113***	0.065***	0.058***	0.046**
	(0.015)	(0.017)	(0.014)	(0.016)
ln Mean HomeAtt$_{Season-1}$		0.198***		0.154***
		(0.036)		(0.038)
ln Mean AwayAtt$_{Season-1}$		0.546***		0.529***
		(0.036)		(0.037)
Title wins of the national team				
Aftertitle3			0.114	0.168*
			(0.068)	(0.075)
Aftertitle6			0.004	0.049
			(0.049)	(0.054)
Stadium quality[a]				
Quality2			−0.135	−0.090
			(0.103)	(0.119)
Quality3			0.058	0.137
			(0.113)	(0.127)
Quality4			−0.215	−0.057
			(0.117)	(0.126)
Quality5			0.102	0.199
			(0.098)	(0.110)
Quality6			0.094	0.094
			(0.085)	(0.098)
Host site characteristics				
RealIncome[b]			0.052	0.063*
			(0.029)	(0.030)
Density			0.000	0.000
			(0.000)	(0.000)
Changes in team affiliations				
Independence			−0.099	0.024
			(0.084)	(0.107)
Switch			0.355**	0.257*
			(0.107)	(0.124)
Team quality				
HomeRank			−0.028***	−0.021**
			(0.006)	(0.007)
AwayRank			−0.050***	−0.030***
			(0.005)	(0.006)

(*continued*)

Table 3.2 (Cont.)

Independent variables	Model 1	Model 2	Model 3	Model 4
	Short-term habit persistence	*Medium-term habit persistence*	*Full model without medium-term habit persistence*	*Full model with medium-term habit persistence*
Team championship chances				
UCS_{Home}			0.012***	0.013***
			(0.002)	(0.002)
UCS_{Away}			0.008***	0.006**
			(0.002)	(0.002)
Uncertainty of matches				
Goliath			0.032	−0.007
			(0.038)	(0.045)
David			-0.053	−0.073
			(0.038)	(0.044)
Scheduling				
Weekend			0.097**	0.155***
			(0.036)	(0.040)
Afternoon			−0.182**	−0.149**
			(0.053)	(0.057)
Evening			0.151	0.155
			(0.082)	(0.090)
Traveling costs				
Distance			−0.018*	−0.020*
			(0.007)	(0.009)
Weather				
Temperature[c]				
Low			0.211***	0.242***
			(0.045)	(0.053)
Warm			0.278***	0.331***
			(0.045)	(0.053)
Very warm			0.293***	0.356***
			(0.060)	(0.069)
Rain[d]				
Slight			−0.019	−0.009
			(0.032)	(0.038)
Moderate			−0.076**	−0.070*
			(0.027)	(0.031)
Strong			−0.036	−0.059
			(0.033)	(0.037)
Season[e]				
1999/00	0.063		0.015	
	(0.068)		(0.061)	
2000/01	0.038		0.074	
	(0.066)		(0.062)	
2001/02 (EURO win)	0.081		0.072	
	(0.066)		(0.067)	
2002/03	0.067		0.070	
	(0.066)		(0.068)	

Table 3.2 (Cont.)

Independent variables	Model 1	Model 2	Model 3	Model 4
	Short-term habit persistence	*Medium-term habit persistence*	*Full model without medium-term habit persistence*	*Full model with medium-term habit persistence*
2003/04 (WC win)	0.359***		0.401***	
	(0.069)		(0.072)	
2004/05	0.298***		0.356***	
	(0.069)		(0.073)	
2005/06 (EURO win)	0.518***		0.575***	
	(0.070)		(0.075)	
2006/07	0.563***		0.625***	
	(0.071)		(0.079)	
2007/08 (WC win)	0.722***		0.815***	
	(0.075)		(0.081)	
2008/09	0.665***		0.760***	
	(0.073)		(0.077)	
2009/10 (EURO win)	0.633***		0.728***	
	(0.073)		(0.076)	
2010/11	0.665***		0.731***	
	(0.073)		(0.075)	
2011/12 ('Home WC)	0.830***		0.900***	
	(0.076)		(0.080)	
2012/13	0.701***		0.716***	
	(0.076)		(0.085)	
2013/14 (EURO win)	0.924***		0.884***	
	(0.079)		(0.091)	
2014/15	0.855***		0.843***	
	(0.079)		(0.091)	
2015/16	0.995***		0.997***	
	(0.083)		(0.098)	
2016/17 (Olympic win)	0.911***		0.840***	
	(0.080)		(0.100)	
Constant	3.368***	−0.247	3.425***	−0.790
	(0.139)	(0.164)	(0.537)	(0.584)
N	2,424	1,611	2,413	1,610
Number of groups	33	23	32	23
Average observation per group	73.5	70.0	75.4	70.0
R^2_{Within}	0.419	0.505	0.549	0.599
$R^2_{Between}$	0.623	0.771	0.618	0.727
$R^2_{Overall}$	0.486	0.598	0.564	0.618

Notes: Dependent variable is home team attendance. Method is fixed effects panel regression. a. Reference category is 'Small sports ground without terraces or spectator facilities'. b. No income statistics were available for the municipality of Leipzig in 2011. c. Reference category is 'Below 0°C'. d. Reference category is 'No rain at all'. e. Reference category is the season of 1998/99. * < 0.05; ** < 0.01; *** < 0.001.

64   *Stadium attendance in women's soccer*

attendance seems to stagnate by this stage. Second, consumer loyalty continues to play an important role for match attendance in the FBL. All habit persistence indicators show significant coefficients. In addition, the model fit indicators evidence that the models perform better in explaining the variance in attendance between the distinct FBL teams than in explaining the variance in attendance between matches of individual FBL teams. Thus, habit persistence and trend indicators alone account for around 62 percent (Model 1) or 77 percent (Model 2) of attendance variance between the distinct FBL teams. The fact that home as well as away match attendances in the preceding match and in the preceding season are significant predictors of attendance, indicates the central role that a loyal fan base plays when it come to attendance numbers for FBL teams. Concerning the impact of short-term habit persistence, the coefficient of home attendance is higher. Regarding medium-term habit persistence, the coefficient for away attendance is higher than for home attendance. This finding suggests that some visiting teams attract systematically larger crowds, either due to their reputation or because they have a substantial number of traveling away fans.

Adding indicators for match quality and host sites characteristics serves to increase the explained overall variance. However, these models do not improve the explained variance between teams but only in attendance for individual teams by 13 percent (Model 3) or by 9 percent (Model 4). Nevertheless, the models suggest that FBL audiences respond to specific quality features of sports entertainment. Thus, visitors are interested in attending fixtures involving better teams, which have a chance to win the championship. In contrast, strongly imbalanced matches do not serve to attract more spectators. Concerning host site characteristics, there is limited evidence that wealthier host sites draw larger audiences (Model 4). Moreover, it seems that switching clubs for economic concerns pays in terms of higher attendance. In contrast, stadium quality does not seem to leave an impact on attendance.

Furthermore, the models support the conclusion that FBL responds to the costs of stadium attendance. Greater distances and, by implication, higher traveling costs reduce attendance. Opportunity costs related to weather and scheduling also matter. Worse weather conditions decrease attendance and there is a scheduling effect as afternoon matches attract significantly less visitors and weekend matches significantly more.

Finally, the performance of the national women's soccer team might play a role for FBL attendance. There is limited evidence for a short-term impact on attendance in one of the models (Model 4) and the coefficients for the year dummies seem to indicate that, in seasons after a tournament victory of the national team, attendance increases.

Accordingly, the seasons following the World Cup victories in 2003 and 2007, the EURO victories in 2005 and 2013, and the victory in the Olympic soccer tournament of 2016 were followed by significant increases in attendance. Yet, the win of the EURO in 2009 did not serve to attract more spectators. Moreover, the fact that FBL attendance grew significantly in the 2011/2012 season might reflect the increased attention for women's soccer generated by the 'home' World Cup, notwithstanding a rather disappointing performance by the national team. However, a general caveat has to be made against such a bold interpretation of the coefficients for the year dummies. The evidence for short-term effects is rather limited and the year dummy coefficients might also reflect effects of changes in league composition.

In order to assess the substantive and practical significance of the findings, elasticities and semi-elasticities were calculated (see Table 3.4). Concerning the elasticities for the habit persistence indicators, the marginal effects calculation makes evident that the marginal effect of a 1 percent increase in home team attendance on attendance for the subsequent match equals only 0.25 percent at maximum (Model 1). If medium-term habit persistence, match, and host site characteristics are taken into account, the effect is reduced to 0.18 percent (Model 3). Medium-term habit effects seem to be less decisive as an increase in average home team attendance in the previous season by 1 percent increases home attendance by 0.20 percent (Model 2) or by 0.16 percent (Model 4). Short-term away attendance seems to have very little effect. At maximum (Model 1), a 1 percent increase in away attendance in the previous match translates into a 0.11 percent increase in home attendance in the subsequent match. More decisive is the impact of medium-term away attendance. A 1 percent increase in average away attendance in the previous seasons results in 0.55 percent (Model 2) or 0.54 percent (Model 4) increase in the subsequent season.

In general, the semi-elasticities on quality and host sites demonstrate the limited relevance of these factors. Thus, a title win by the German national team increases stadium attendance in the first three matchdays of a season only by 2.7 percent (Model 4). An improvement of the home team's league ranking by one rank increases attendance by 0.5 or 0.3 percent, an equal improvement of the away team's ranking increases attendance by 0.8 or 0.5 percent. Host site characteristics appear also to play only a minor role. According to Model 4, a one-thousand Euro increase in regional income serves to increase attendance by 2.7 percent. In contrast, switching to wealthier clubs relates to a rather substantial marginal attendance growth by almost 6.0 percent (Model 3) or 4.2 percent (Model 4). Moreover, the semi-elasticities demonstrate

Table 3.3 Semi-elasticities and elasticities for demand for Frauen-Bundesliga matches

Independent variables	Model 1	Model 2	Model 3	Model 4
	Short-term habit persistence	Medium-term habit persistence	Full model without medium-term habit persistence	Full model with medium-term habit persistence
Elasticities (percentage increase)				
Habit persistence indicators				
ln Attendance$_{t-1}$	0.254***	0.220***	0.185***	0.178***
ln AwayAttendance$_{t-1}$	0.113***	0.065***	0.058***	0.045**
ln Mean HomeAtt$_{Season-1}$		0.199***		0.155***
ln MeanAwayAtt$_{Season-1}$		0.556***		0.539***
Semi-elasticities (percentage increase)				
Title wins of the national team				
Aftertitle3			1.918	2.737*
Aftertitle6			0.100	0.803
Stadium quality[a]				
Quality2			–2.274	–1.489
Quality3			1.005	2.224
Quality4			–3.536	–0.896
Quality5			1.715	3.252
Quality6			1.511	1.511
Host site characteristics				
RealIncome[b]			0.803	1.005*
Density			0.000	0.000
Changes in team affiliations				
Independence			–1.587	0.401
Switch			5.971**	4.185*
Team quality				
HomeRank			–0.499***	–0.300**
AwayRank			–0.797***	–0.499***
Team championship chances				
UCS$_{Home}$			0.200***	0.200***
UCS$_{Away}$			0.100***	0.100**

Table 3.3 (Cont.)

Independent variables	Model 1	Model 2	Model 3	Model 4
	Short-term habit persistence	*Medium-term habit persistence*	*Full model without medium-term habit persistence*	*Full model with medium-term habit persistence*
Uncertainty of matches				
Goliath			0.501	−0.100
David			−0.896	−1.193
Scheduling				
Weekend			1.613**	2.532***
Afternoon			−2.955**	−2.371**
Evening			2.532	2.532
Traveling costs				
Distance			−0.300*	-0.300*
Weather				
Temperature[c]				
Low			3.562***	4.081***
Warm			4.707***	5.548***
Very warm			5.022***	5.971***
Rain[d]				
Slight			−0.300	−0.100
Moderate			−1.292**	−1.094*
Strong			−0.598	−0.995
Season[e]				
1999/00	1.106		0.300	
2000/01	0.702		1.308	
2001/02 (EURO win)	1.410		1.308	
2002/03	1.207		1.207	
2003/04 (WC win)	6.396***		7.251***	
2004/05	5.338***		6.396***	
2005/06 (EURO win)	9.199***		10.296***	
2006/07	10.076***		11.182***	
2007/08 (WC win)	12.862***		14.568***	
2008/09	11.851***		13.655***	
2009/10 (EURO win)	11.293***		13.088***	
2010/11	11.851***		13.088***	
2011/12 ('Home WC)	14.798***		16.183***	
2012/13	12.524***		12.862***	
2013/14 (EURO win)	16.416***		15.835***	

(continued)

68 *Stadium attendance in women's soccer*

Table 3.3 (Cont.)

Independent variables	Model 1	Model 2	Model 3	Model 4
	Short-term habit persistence	Medium-term habit persistence	Full model without medium-term habit persistence	Full model with medium-term habit persistence
2014/15	15.258***		15.142***	
2015/16	17.704***		17.821***	
2016/17 (Olympic win)	16.183***		15.027***	

Notes: a. Reference category is 'Small sports ground without terraces or spectator facilities'. b. No income statistics were available for the municipality of Leipzig in 2011. c. Reference category is 'Below 0°C'. d. Reference category is 'No rain at all'. e. Reference category is the season of 1998/99. * < 0.05; ** < 0.01; *** < 0.001.

the importance of weather conditions and opportunity costs. Weather conditions, in particular temperature, appear to exert stronger effects on attendance than the quality of the involved teams. The same conclusion applies to scheduling effects. Weekend fixtures attract 1.6 percent (Model 3) or 2.5 percent (Model 4) more visitors, whereas afternoon fixtures reduce attendance by almost 3.0 percent (Model 3) or 2.4 percent (Model 4). Finally, the semi-elasticities show again that the increase in attendance is not strictly linear. Whereas the average marginal effect of the 2016/2017 season in comparison to the reference season of 1998/1999 equals 16.2 percent (Model 1) or 15.0 percent (Model 3), it should be noticed that these models do not include medium-habit indicators, implying that short-term seasonal effects are slightly overestimated.

Conclusion

Women's first-tier league soccer has been characterized as German women's soccer's 'problem child' (Hennies & Meuren, 2011: 165). Given the success of German women's soccer teams in international club competitions, the characterization might appear exaggerated. However, the results presented here suggest that the viability of (semi-)professional women's soccer is still problematic. Not surprisingly, the data show a substantial gap between attendance for first-tier men's soccer and the FBL. Whereas attendance for women's top division matches has increased over the period examined, the data do not support the idea that attendance figures for women's and men's soccer will converge, in the near future in particular, as there exists no strong and continuous linear growth trend. Hence, the findings provide little reason for the optimism that the future of soccer will be female.

Concerning the second question of whether women's league soccer represents primarily a niche product, the analyses suggest that fan loyalty continues to play a dominant role and that the very quality features, which have been commonly found to drive stadium attendance in professional sports, play only a secondary role. Thus, the FBL represents still a niche product targeting mainly diehard fans. However, comparing these recent findings with the ones of the predecessor study on FBL attendance serves to qualify these. Whereas previous analyses, which covered the seasons from 1998/1999 to 2011/2012, found similar results (Meier, Konjer, & Leinwather, 2016), the dominant role of habit persistence seems to have declined during more recent seasons. The FBL might attract new customers who are less dedicated and respond more strongly to quality features as well as opportunity costs. A further contrast to the previous results, also, is that changes in team affiliations now seem to have translated into higher attendance numbers.

Nevertheless, in terms of practical implications, the results presented provide little guidance on DFB policies for increasing FBL attendance. Whereas FBL attendance responds to quality features specific to sports entertainment, the marginal effects are small. Accordingly, attendance increases with the sporting quality of the home team and the away team, as reflected in league rankings. Moreover, stadium attendance increases with seasonal uncertainty, that is, matches involving teams that have a chance to win the championship attract more visitors. However, given the rather small marginal effects, the results do not suggest a strong need for policies to improve competitive balance within the FBL. Yet, match outcome uncertainty appears to play no role for FBL attendance. The finding that seasonal uncertainty matters for attendance is relevant insofar as the FBL represents a rather imbalanced league in which the top teams heavily concentrate national playing talent.

Surprisingly, the considerable improvements in venue quality over the years do not seem to affect stadium attendance substantially, even though venue quality has been substantially lower in the FBL than in men's top soccer. By implication, providing women's first division teams with top-notch venues is not the most urgent policy to be adopted. Moreover, more urban host sites do not attract more visitors. Whereas the analyses indicate that attendance increases with higher regional income, the finding should be cautiously interpreted as measurement is suboptimal and there is a general increase in regional income across all host sites. Yet, whereas the previous study concluded that changes

70 *Stadium attendance in women's soccer*

in club affiliations were not well received by FBL visitors, the consideration of more recent seasons shows that the women's team might be encouraged to join the larger men's clubs in order to benefit from a more professional approach and higher spending power. Moreover, the evidence for significant temperature and scheduling effects could serve to inspire the DFB to reflect on changes in the match calendar.

Nevertheless, the results appear to indicate that the DFB has not much choice in policy when it comes to increasing FBL attendance. With the exception of the first World Cup win in 2003, even the impressive performances of the national women's soccer team did not affect FBL attendance. However, although the more aggressive marketing campaign for the 2011 World Cup might have served to attract more visitors in comparison to the preceding seasons, where attendances were at least stagnating, the increase has been far from impressive and has proven to be not sustainable. Thus, the DFB might decide to continue to increase general awareness for women's soccer by stronger marketing efforts but such measures have to be complemented by the local policies of the FBL teams in order to expand their fan base. Women's league soccer still represents a niche product primarily targeting diehard fans even though average attendances are slowly increasing. Accordingly, the future of FBL attendance depends on the teams' ability to build a sustainable fan base.

Notes

1 The UEFA Women's Champions League (UEFA Women's Cup until the 2008/2009 season) has been won four times by 1. FFC Frankfurt, twice by 1. FFC Turbine Potsdam and VfL Wolfsburg, and once by FCR 2001 Duisburg.
2 1. FFC Frankfurt and 1. FFC Turbine Potsdam won the FBL six times, VfL Wolfsburg three times, FC Bayern München twice and FCR 2001 Duisburg once.
3 The single match day ticket prices range from EUR 3.50 charged by SC Freiburg to EUR 10 charged by Werder Bremen. There is no differentiated pricing strategy for FBL matches in contrast to first-tier matches for men's soccer. Hence, for SC Freiburg men's matches, ticket prices range from EUR 16 to EUR 72, and for Werder Bremen from EUR 15 to EUR 70.

4 The popularity of the women's national soccer team

Introduction

When the West German men's national soccer team quite unexpectedly won the 1954 World Cup, a national euphoria broke out. After the disastrous defeat in World War II and the Nazi atrocities, the World Cup win gave rise to a feeling of 'We are someone again'. Some commentators even went so far as to characterize the 'Miracle of Berne' as the true birth of the Federal Republic (Brüggemeier, 2004, 2006). The victory also inspired patriotic feelings behind the iron curtain. East German radio listeners reacted quite angrily when the East German radio reporter avoided any partisanship for the West German team (Becker & Buss, 2006). Since then, the German men's national soccer team has acquired the status of an almost uncontested national icon. Its appeal has further increased since the team has become multi-ethnic in its composition (Meier & Leinwather, 2013).[1]

Hence, matches played by the men's national soccer team reach impressive audience figures. Some 61.60 million German viewers or 85.30 percent of the entire audience potential watched at least one match of the 2014 World Cup (Gerhard & Zubayr, 2014) and 59.79 million viewers or 79.6 percent watched at least one match of the 2016 EURO tournament (Gerhard & Geese, 2016). Given its impressive popularity, national team soccer has been characterized as the last remaining 'campfire' around which an increasingly fragmentized society gathers (Meier & Hagenah, 2016). Accordingly, it should not come as a surprise that the German listed event regulations ban the 'siphoning' of the men's national team's matches to pay TV and have made free-to-air broadcasts compulsory (Meier, 2004).

In contrast, women's soccer faced great difficulties in making it onto German TV screens at all. Hence, when the DFB finally lifted its ban on women's soccer in 1970, TV presenter Wim Thölke used the occasion

72   *Popularity of women's national soccer*

to ridicule female soccer players in the popular sport show 'Aktuelles Sportstudio'. Thölke's mocking culminated in the not very subtle, yet hard to translate, wordplay 'Decken, decken! Nicht Tischdecken' ('Marking, marking! Not tablesetting') (ZDFsport, 2013). Obviously, Thölke invoked the long-established stereotypical belief in a general ineptitude of women who play soccer. They were depicted as being incapable of executing a basic organized defensive strategy, such as man-to-man marking, since their true talents were in household chores.

Such an openly derogatory attitude might have been exceptional.[2] Yet, German TV stations ignored women's soccer for a long time. Even though German TV audiences awarded the prestigious 'Goal of the Month' trophy for the first time to a female soccer player as early as 1974 (Hennies & Meuren, 2011: 55), an entire women's soccer match was not telecast on German TV screens before Germany hosted the European Competition for Women's Football in 1989. For the period from 1995 to 2011, Meier and Leinwather (2012) found that every match of the men's national team was telecast but only 61.6 percent of the matches of the women's national team. Moreover, the major public service networks, 'Das Erste' (ARD1) and the 'Zweites Deutsches Fernsehen' (ZDF), relegated telecasts of women's soccer to minor public services stations with a lower technical reach and limited audience potential. The neglect for women's national soccer only substantially changed when Chancellor Gerhard Schröder demanded that the public service broadcasters (PSBs) increase TV coverage of women's soccer after the triumph of the women's team in the UEFA women's EURO 2005 tournament (Frankfurter Allgemeine Zeitung, 2005). Whereas the PSBs followed up the request, commercial networks did not even bid for the broadcasting rights for the women's team.

Given the long history of discrimination, under-resourcing, and ignorance, it is hardly surprising that the women's team continues to be less popular than the men's team (Meier & Leinwather, 2012). Accordingly, this chapter will not compare the popularity of both teams but, rather, will trace how the popularity of the women's national team has evolved. Since the 'home' EURO tournament of 1989, the women's national soccer team has served as women's soccer's most visible outlet (Hennies & Meuren, 2011: 131). In contrast to women's league soccer, the national team has attracted substantial stadium crowds and media attention.

The higher public attention for the women's national team partly reflects the serious promotional efforts made by the DFB. However, these campaigns have proven to be controversial. The DFB, as with other soccer governing bodies (Fink, 2015), supported a more feminine

Popularity of women's national soccer 73

or even eroticized image of the sport in order to increase its appeal for male audiences. There is certainly some (albeit cynical) rationality behind such considerations. The lesbian or 'butch' image, which women's soccer acquired in many European countries, has been perceived as reducing the sports' appeal to male consumers (cf. Harris, 2005: 187). Moreover, since the sports media primarily cater to the (perceived) needs of a predominantly male audience, female athletes have been often depicted in sexualized ways (Vincent et al., 2007; Cranmer et al., 2014; Kim & Sagas, 2014). In addition, physical attractiveness has been found to increase the popularity of female athletes (Fink et al., 2004; Cunningham et al., 2008; Konjer et al., 2019). The strategy of eroticized marketing became evident in particular on the occasion of the 2011 World Cup, which was hosted by Germany. In the perception of the DFB, the 'home' World Cup competition represented a unique opportunity to create for the women's national team an unprecedented level of media attention and stadium attendance. To achieve these aims, the DFB chose the official advertisement slogan '20elf von seiner schönsten Seite' ('20eleven from its most beautiful side'). Not surprisingly, soccer academics and women's soccer activists have heavily criticized the alleged 'sell-out' of women's soccer, in particular after some players were presented as catwalk models (Schaaf, 2014). The marketing strategy was ethically questionable, as research has indicated that female athletes prefer to be depicted in a non-sexualized way (Krane et al., 2010; Kane et al., 2013). Moreover, various groups of sports consumers do favor a non-sexualized presentation of females (Kane & Maxwell, 2011).

Other elements of the 2011 promotional campaign were perceived as too aggressive. Several members of the national team endorsed telecasts of the World Cup under the slogan 'Dritte Plätze sind was für Männer' ('Third places are only for men'). By alluding to the third place achieved by the men's national team at the 2010 FIFA World Cup in South Africa, the slogan seemed to derogate the men's achievement and implied that the women's team would win the home World Cup for sure. Not surprisingly, the campaign backfired when the German team was beaten by Japan in the quarter-final (Frankfurter Allgemeine Zeitung, 2011). In actual fact, the early elimination in the 'home' World Cup represented the worst result a German women's soccer team had ever achieved since the creation of the competition in 1991 and provoked intense debate about the team's future (Hennies & Meuren, 2011: 402). In athletic terms, the 2011 World Cup marked a turning point for the German national team as it indicated that international women's soccer had become more competitive. Since then, the German team has been able to deliver top performances but has been unable to maintain its

74 *Popularity of women's national soccer*

dominance. Although Germany won the UEFA Women's Euro 2013 and the Olympic soccer tournament of 2016, the team was beaten by the U.S. in the semifinal of the 2015 FIFA World Cup and by Denmark in the quarter-final of the UEFA Women's Euro 2017. After a string of defeats in the SheBelieves Cup, the coach was fired and the team entered a process of transformation. Although the German team managed to qualify for the 2019 World Cup, hosted by France, it delivered again disappointing performances and was beaten by Sweden in the quarter-final. Several German soccer officials complained that Germany has lost its leading role in women's soccer and has been overtaken by other nations (Meuren, 2018, 2019).

It is relevant to state here, however, that notwithstanding a disappointing team performance, the 'home' World Cup created unprecedented public attention for women's soccer (Nieland, 2013; Schaaf, 2013, 2014). Despite the criticism of a 'sell-out' in women's soccer, this chapter studies the popularity of the women's national soccer team. Popularity represents a prerequisite for the future development of women's soccer in terms of professionalization prospects. Popularity defines access to financial resources. Popular sports can benefit from marketing broadcasting or sponsorship rights; they might also enjoy better access to government subsidies. As Williams (2003: 8) has emphasized, women's soccer's access to any kind of equality remains hampered by structures that reinforce female soccer as primarily an amateur and voluntary leisure activity. Of course, it can be questioned whether professionalization is a desirable goal for women's soccer, as claimed by Williams (2003: 148), since it might replace traditional amateur sports models that rely on social cohesion and voluntarism (Kjær & Agergaard, 2013), or may weaken the association of women's soccer with feminism and LGBT identities (Caudwell, 2006). Nevertheless, understanding determinants of popularity might also be relevant for participation in women's soccer although the inspirational effects of elite soccer should not be exaggerated (Wicker & Frick, 2015; Frick & Wicker, 2016).

Modernization of gender-role attitudes and women's sport

The 'future of soccer is feminine' *leitmotif* of this book suggests that the popularity of the women's national soccer team should increase over time. This prediction is not solely inspired by Sepp Blatter's claim but also rooted in theoretical reasoning. In particular McCabe (2007, 2008) has provided evidence that people who hold more egalitarian gender-role orientations are more prone to being fans of women's sport.

Accordingly, the popularity of women's sport should benefit from a modernization of gender-role attitudes.

In Germany—in particular in the more socially conservative Western parts—there is substantial evidence for such a trend among younger cohorts. Moreover, the traditional male breadwinner model that dominates in West German families has eroded due to a deregulation of labor market laws and a reform of welfare benefits. As a result, female part-time work has turned into an increasingly important source of family income (Trappe et al., 2015). Admittedly, the extent to which these changes in gender-role attitudes have translated into actual changes in behavior is controversial. Hence, men's role as the primary breadwinner has only partly been challenged and family labor remains unequally distributed (Pollmann-Schult & Reynolds, 2017). Traditional gender ideology continues to be present even in self-declared equal responsibility partnerships (Haase et al., 2016), and the provision of public childcare has not encouraged more female labor force participation (Busse & Gathmann, 2018).

Notwithstanding the tensions between changed attitudes and actual behavior, the more gender-equal social climate in post-reunification Germany should favor a growing popularity of the women's national soccer team. Moreover, the women's national soccer team should be more popular among younger cohorts who have been socialized in a more gender-equal social climate. In addition, the fact that Germany allows for tracking the impact of different gender regimes on the popularity of women's soccer will be taken into account.

As elaborated in the introductory chapter, gender policies adopted in both Germanys differed quite substantially before reunification. West Germany implemented a highly unequal gender regime that discouraged mothers in particular from participating in the labor force (Konietzka & Kreyenfeld, 2002). In contrast, the East German communists officially promoted gender equality and encouraged high levels of female labor force participation, even for mothers. Thus, East Germany had the highest female employment rate in the world (Lee et al., 2007). Both regimes have left lasting legacies. East Germans hold more egalitarian sex role attitudes and support the labor force participation of mothers (Geisler & Kreyenfeld, 2005; Bauernschuster & Rainer, 2011). Still, labor market participation of East German women continues to be higher (Adler & Brayfield, 1997; Konietzka & Kreyenfeld, 2002; Lee et al., 2007; Hanel & Riphan, 2011).

However, the higher gender equality in East Germany did not translate into gender equality in soccer. Soccer remained a highly gendered sport in East Germany because it was irrelevant for the Olympic

76 *Popularity of women's national soccer*

medal record. The neglect for the sport is particularly reflected in the fact that an East German women's national soccer team did not exist before 1990. When the team was finally created, it played only one match, due to reunification (Linne, 2011, 2014). These differences and tensions in gender regimes raise the question of whether they have left a lasting impact on the popularity of the women's national soccer team. Accordingly, this chapter will examine trends in the TV coverage of matches of the women's national soccer team in different German federal states over a period of 22 years.

Analyzing the popularity of the women's national soccer team

The use of TV audience figures as a measure of popularity and consumer demand has become a common approach among sports sociologists and economists (Hausman & Leonard, 1997; Kanazawa & Funk, 2001; Forrest et al., 2005; Paul & Weinbach, 2007; Buraimo, 2008; Nüesch & Franck, 2009; Tainsky, 2010; Feddersen & Rott, 2011; Tainsky & McEvoy, 2012; Meier & Leinwather, 2013). Whereas the analysis of TV ratings comes with a number of methodological advantages in comparison to the study of attendance figures (e.g., Forrest et al., 2005; Tainsky & McEvoy, 2012), TV consumption and stadium attendance differ in important respects. In contrast to stadium visitors, TV consumers are less likely to behave as loyal fans and are more interested in the sporting relevance and quality of sporting contests, as well as in uncertain outcomes (e.g., Baimbridge et al., 1996; Forrest et al., 2005; Buraimo & Simmons, 2008; Mongeon & Winfree, 2012).

The current study relies on a unique dataset of all live telecasts of matches of the women's national soccer team conducted by the 'Gesellschaft für Konsumforschung' (GfK). The dataset includes ratings for all 250 matches of the women's national soccer team between January 1, 1995 and December 31, 2017. In order to address the questions guiding this chapter, the ratings have been broken down into several regional and demographic subcategories.

In order to account for a possible influence of policy legacies in reunified Germany, the TV ratings for the matches were first stratified on the basis of the 16 federal states. In addition, TV ratings were differentiated according to biological sex. Using such a binary gender classification is slightly over-simplistic since psychological research has demonstrated that gender traits and gender-role orientations might qualify as more valid predictors of interest in women's sport (Wann & Waddill, 2003; McCabe, 2007, 2008). However, TV ratings data leave little alternative to stratifying the data according to the audiences' biological sex.

Moreover, as a matter of fact, sport consumption has remained highly gendered and the sports-viewing behavior of women and men continues to differ substantially (e.g., Gantz & Wenner, 1991; Gantz et al., 2006; Meier, Strauß, & Riedl, 2017). Since it has been assumed that younger cohorts should be more prone to watching women's sport, the following socio-demographic groups were defined: 'Younger women': women up to 50 years, 'Older women': women 51 years and older, 'Older men': men up to 50 years, and 'Older men': men 51 years and older.

With regard to determinants of demand for matches of the women's national soccer team, the account again follows canonical approaches of empirical sports economics, which have demonstrated that specific quality factors determine the demand for sports entertainment. These quality features are sporting relevance, athletic quality, and uncertainty of outcome (see, for excellent reviews, Borland & MacDonald, 2003; Buraimo, 2008; García & Rodríguez, 2009).

Sporting relevance refers usually to the prestige of a competition and/or its status in the competitive hierarchy of a specific sport (e.g., Czarnitzki & Stadtmann, 2002; García & Rodríguez, 2002; Berri et al., 2004; Forrest et al., 2005; Buraimo & Simmons, 2008). A particular advantage of national team soccer is the existence of a clear competitive hierarchy in which continental championships, such as the UEFA EURO tournaments, and ultimately world championships, that is, the FIFA World Cup, occupy the top echelons. Moreover, in women's soccer, Olympic tournaments seem to enjoy a specific prestige. In addition to indicators for tournaments, relevance is defined by the tournament stages. As a result, a set of dummy variables was created in order to account for sporting relevance: *Qualification* refers to qualification matches for EURO and World Cup tournaments. *Olympic group* includes all group matches played during the Olympic soccer tournaments and *Olympic final* refers to the advanced stages of the Olympic soccer tournaments. The dummy variables coded for the EURO and World Cup matches follow the same logic. Accordingly, the dataset includes the dummy variables *Euro group*, *Euro final*, *World Group* and *World Cup final*.

With regard to athletic quality, sport economists have demonstrated that the quality of the involved teams, as measured by win percentages and team rankings, exerts a strong influence on consumer demand (e.g., Forrest et al., 2005; Buraimo & Simmons, 2008; Tainsky & Winfree, 2010). As shown in the introductory chapter, scholars of international women's soccer have relied on FIFA's ranking system for measuring the athletic quality of national teams. Unfortunately, FIFA rankings for women's national soccer teams have only been available since

78 *Popularity of women's national soccer*

July 16, 2003. Moreover, there has been little variance in Germany's FIFA ranking. The lack of data also poses problems for examining the long-debated relevance of outcome uncertainty for sports consumers (Rottenberg, 1956; Neale, 1964; Szymanski, 2003; Pawlowski, 2013). Historical betting odds are rarely available for matches of women's soccer teams. Therefore, this chapter also uses a number of dummy variables on opponent quality as a proxy for match outcome uncertainty.

Matches of the women's national soccer team have been exclusively broadcast by free-to-air public service networks. Free-to-air TV telecasts represent a 'low barrier' venue for occasional sports spectators who face no costs other than opportunity costs and can revise their entertainment choices immediately by pushing a button on the remote control (e.g., Forrest & Simmons, 2006; Simmons, 2006; Berkowitz et al., 2011). Opportunity costs for free-to-air telecasts are usually measured by indicator for scheduling and weather conditions. As measures of the public visibility of the team, dummies for home matches (*Home*) and telecasts on major networks (*Major Networks*) were included.

According to the 'future of soccer is feminine' *leitmotif* of the book, one of the key questions addressed in this chapter is whether the popularity of the women's national soccer team increases over time. Therefore, the years in which the matches were broadcast served as the basis for the creation of a trend indicator. However, given the fact that the 'home' World Cup of 2011 created unusual media attention and might have had a rather ambiguous effect on the popularity of women's soccer, a semi-parametric modeling approach seemed more appropriate. Accordingly, years have been coded as a set of dummy variables.

Furthermore, in order to examine the potential socialization effects of the different gender regimes in West and East Germany, a simple dummy variable for East Germany was created (*East*). To answer the questions of whether there is convergence or divergence between TV consumption patterns in West and East Germany, interaction effects between these year dummy variables and *East* were modeled. As the dataset is characterized by a complex structure, a generalized estimating equation (GEE) approach for panel data was employed.

Growth, cycles, peaks, and stagnation

The development of national TV market shares across the entire German population for the matches of the women's national team shows that the ratings for the team have varied substantially and have been characterized by a cyclical pattern according to which major tournaments such as the World Cup, the Olympics, and the EURO attract larger audiences.

Popularity of women's national soccer 79

With around a 60.1 percent market share, the ratings reached an all-time high during the opening match of the 'home' World Cup in 2011 (*Germany v. Canada*, June 26, 2011). The second most popular match was the quarter-final of the 'home' World Cup in which the German team was defeated early on by the later to be crowned world champion, Japan (*Germany v. Japan*, July 9, 2011). The figure also makes evident that, after the unprecedented attention during the 2011 World Cup, audience figures during the big tournaments seemed to be declining. Audience shares even reached their all-time low (1.0 percent) after 2011 when the German team played against Norway during the Algarve Cup of 2014 (*Germany v. Norway*, March 10, 2014). However, this all-time low and the decline of ratings does not necessarily support the idea that the promotional campaign for the 2011 World Cup backfired on the team, as hosting the mega-soccer event created exceptional attention for women's soccer. Moreover, it has to be taken into account that the Algarve Cup match was only telecast by the special interest network 'Eurosport' and not by a major public service broadcaster. Nevertheless, the data seem to defy the idea of a clear trend toward a growing popularity of the women's national soccer team.

Comparing average TV ratings across German regions, and the four demographic groups defined, proves to be highly instructive.

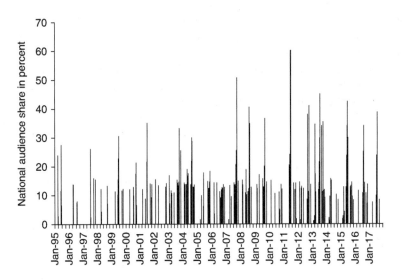

Figure 4.1 TV ratings for matches of the women's national soccer team from 1995 to 2017

Source: Media Control/GfK.

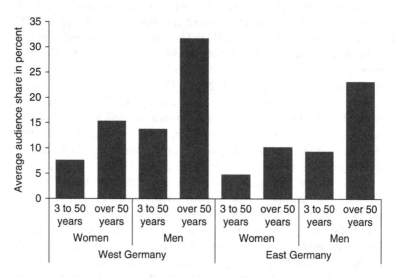

Figure 4.2 TV ratings for matches of the women's national soccer team from 1995 to 2017

Note: N = 15,998 observations.
Source: Media Control/GfK.

First, there is a visible regional divide according to which the women's national soccer team is substantially less popular in East Germany. Furthermore, men are more likely to watch matches of the women's national soccer team than women. Finally, the age effect works against theoretical expectations as the audience of the women's national soccer team is rather more composed of older than of younger people (see Figure 4.2).

A simple ANOVA, with the square root transformed *Ratings* as the dependent variable and *East*, *Sex*, and *Age* as independent variables, reveals that all of these differences are statistically significant. In terms of effect size, *Age* has the strongest impact on audience shares followed by *Sex* while *East* exerts only a small effect (Table 4.1).

Several multivariate models were calculated for the different socio-demographic groups. Since FIFA rankings for the women's national teams have only been available since 2003, the models were estimated with and without opponent quality indicators (Table 4.2, Models 1 to 2, and Table 4.3, Models 5 to 8).

With regard to the key questions of this chapter, the models for all socio-demographic groups suggest that, over the entire period examined, the women's national soccer team has become more popular.

Table 4.1 MANOVA of TV ratings for matches of the women's national soccer team

Independent variables	df	F	η^2	P
East	1	604.30	0.036	> 0.001
Sex	1	2,636.85	0.142	> 0.001
Age	1	3,876.45	0.195	> 0.001
Model	3	2,372.61	0.308	> 0.001

Notes: Dependent variable is *sqrt Ratings*; 15,998 observations; adjusted $R^2 = 0.308$.

Table 4.2 TV ratings for matches of the women's national soccer team from 1995 to 2017

Independent variables	Model 1	Model 2	Model 3	Model 4
	Younger women	Older women	Younger men	Older men
Athletic relevance[a]				
Qualification	0.390***	0.243***	0.336***	0.442***
	(0.079)	(0.059)	(0.074)	(0.056)
Olympic Group	1.672***	1.649***	2.149***	1.826***
	(0.127)	(0.100)	(0.124)	(0.101)
Olympic Final	2.041***	1.717***	2.251***	1.648***
	(0.116)	(0.096)	(0.118)	(0.099)
EURO Group	0.043	0.433***	0.327**	0.847***
	(0.122)	(0.099)	(0.121)	(0.095)
EURO Final	1.411***	1.516***	1.621***	1.896***
	(0.111)	(0.093)	(0.112)	(0.091)
World Group	2.294***	1.462***	2.042***	1.593***
	(0.100)	(0.085)	(0.097)	(0.086)
World Final	2.644***	2.009***	2.587***	2.323***
	(0.100)	(0.085)	(0.099)	(0.086)
East[b]	−1.309***	−0.652*	−0.845*	−0.997**
	(0.323)	(0.288)	(0.328)	(0.294)
Year[c]				
1996	0.213	-0.186	0.938**	0.904**
	(0.416)	(0.408)	(0.340)	(0.273)
1997	0.783**	1.159***	1.398***	1.350***
	(0.256)	(0.212)	(0.251)	(0.206)
1998	1.324**	1.318***	1.926***	1.560***
	(0.383)	(0.297)	(0.340)	(0.269)
1999	0.173	0.379	1.544***	0.984***
	(0.210)	(0.206)	(0.214)	(0.195)
2000	0.288	0.702**	1.084***	0.654**
	(0.265)	(0.216)	(0.249)	(0.211)

(continued)

Table 4.2 (Cont.)

Independent variables	Model 1	Model 2	Model 3	Model 4
	Younger women	Older women	Younger men	Older men
2001	1.299***	1.369***	1.963***	1.647***
	(0.227)	(0.199)	(0.231)	(0.194)
2002	1.413***	1.610***	2.323***	1.817***
	(0.293)	(0.234)	(0.266)	(0.227)
2003	0.913***	1.030***	1.524***	0.944***
	(0.184)	(0.181)	(0.203)	(0.181)
2004	1.413***	1.555***	1.837***	1.579***
	(0.195)	(0.186)	(0.213)	(0.187)
2005	1.675***	1.628***	2.064***	1.567***
	(0.239)	(0.215)	(0.250)	(0.209)
2006	1.337***	1.364***	1.605***	1.283***
	(0.222)	(0.201)	(0.235)	(0.198)
2007	1.402***	1.602***	1.693***	1.563***
	(0.177)	(0.178)	(0.201)	(0.178)
2008	1.515***	2.020***	2.027***	1.841***
	(0.197)	(0.185)	(0.213)	(0.186)
2009	1.724***	1.654***	1.858***	1.561***
	(0.199)	(0.186)	(0.216)	(0.185)
2010	1.681***	1.426***	1.564***	1.155***
	(0.263)	(0.233)	(0.287)	(0.233)
2011	2.449***	2.150***	2.698***	2.044***
	(0.170)	(0.176)	(0.195)	(0.179)
2012	2.286***	1.870***	2.488***	1.590***
	(0.195)	(0.194)	(0.215)	(0.195)
2013	1.842***	1.492***	2.085***	1.456***
	(0.180)	(0.178)	(0.200)	(0.178)
2014	0.833**	0.885***	0.681*	0.617***
	(0.287)	(0.224)	(0.308)	(0.218)
2015	0.990***	1.503***	1.517***	1.078***
	(0.172)	(0.176)	(0.198)	(0.179)
2016	1.538***	1.118***	0.932***	0.636**
	(0.194)	(0.191)	(0.223)	(0.193)
2017	1.784***	1.476***	1.586***	1.102***
	(0.206)	(0.199)	(0.232)	(0.203)
East * Year				
1996	−0.644	1.088	0.003	0.413
	(0.852)	(0.632)	(0.678)	(0.494)
1997	1.142*	−0.359	0.517	0.447
	(0.475)	(0.397)	(0.445)	(0.367)
1998	0.691	0.001	0.291	−0.400
	(0.887)	(0.586)	(0.664)	(0.545)
1999	0.458	−0.142	−0.303	0.142
	(0.460)	(0.397)	(0.421)	(0.364)

Table 4.2 (Cont.)

Independent variables	Model 1	Model 2	Model 3	Model 4
	Younger women	Older women	Younger men	Older men
2000	−1.221	−0.671	−0.276	0.305
	(0.508)	(0.436)	(0.471)	(0.379)
2001	0.842*	0.160	0.116	0.641
	(0.421)	(0.345)	(0.407)	(0.338)
2002	0.889	−0.055	−0.024	−0.105
	(0.604)	(0.446)	(0.525)	(0.432)
2003	0.604	−0.282	−0.270	0.367
	(0.384)	(0.335)	(0.387)	(0.330)
2004	0.954	−0.360	0.090	−0.031
	(0.365)	(0.329)	(0.373)	(0.331)
2005	0.864	−0.214	0.212	0.219
	(0.466)	(0.404)	(0.463)	(0.378)
2006	0.620	0.031	0.220	−0.010
	(0.479)	(0.367)	(0.443)	(0.365)
2007	0.290	−0.164	0.098	0.025
	(0.372)	(0.324)	(0.373)	(0.329)
2008	0.099	−0.312	0.164	−0.177
	(0.387)	(0.329)	(0.366)	(0.328)
2009	0.894*	−0.418	0.244	−0.147
	(0.378)	(0.334)	(0.383)	(0.332)
2010	0.881	0.087	0.444	0.250
	(0.508)	(0.421)	(0.519)	(0.425)
2011	0.314	−0.317	−0.096	0.238
	(0.347)	(0.320)	(0.358)	(0.327)
2012	0.590	−0.186	0.138	−0.037
	(0.392)	(0.359)	(0.396)	(0.364)
2013	0.607	−0.208	0.271	0.048
	(0.354)	(0.321)	(0.358)	(0.324)
2014	1.143*	0.256	0.339	−0.008
	(0.551)	(0.409)	(0.613)	(0.419)
2015	0.785*	0.158	−0.090	0.338
	(0.363)	(0.319)	(0.378)	(0.330)
2016	0.920*	0.166	−0.097	0.415
	(0.360)	(0.329)	(0.401)	(0.341)
2017	0.681	0.024	0.193	0.054
	(0.405)	(0.358)	(0.424)	(0.374)
Home[d]	0.106	0.197***	0.096	0.309***
	(0.065)	(0.050)	(0.062)	(0.050)
Major[e]	1.660***	2.335***	2.207***	2.613***
	(0.135)	(0.125)	(0.134)	(0.101)
Weekend[f]	0.433***	0.377***	0.128*	−0.060
	(0.049)	(0.042)	(0.051)	(0.043)

(continued)

Table 4.2 (Cont.)

Independent variables	Model 1	Model 2	Model 3	Model 4
	Younger women	*Older women*	*Younger men*	*Older men*
Prime Time[g]	1.174***	0.737***	1.460***	0.423***
	(0.071)	(0.069)	(0.075)	(0.071)
Season[h]				
Summer	0.293**	0.103	0.134	0.111
	(0.095)	(0.070)	(0.089)	(0.067)
Fall	–0.168*	–0.099	–0.078	–0.072
	(0.081)	(0.060)	(0.076)	(0.057)
Winter	0.125	0.221	0.097	–0.014
	(0.153)	(0.114)	(0.141)	(0.112)
Temperature[i]				
Low	–0.905***	–0.581***	–0.994***	–0.480**
	(0.169)	(0.155)	(0.170)	(0.145)
Warm	–0.931***	–0.516**	–1.050***	–0.507**
	(0.171)	(0.156)	(0.172)	(0.146)
Very warm	–0.829***	–0.469**	–0.925***	–0.434**
	(0.177)	(0.161)	(0.178)	(0.152)
Rain[j]				
Slight	0.332***	0.134	0.292**	0.130
	(0.087)	(0.075)	(0.087)	(0.073)
Moderate	0.130	–0.171	–0.076	–0.025
	(0.100)	(0.094)	(0.106)	(0.090)
Strong	–0.011	0.285	0.101	0.368*
	(0.230)	(0.182)	(0.232)	(0.184)
Constant	–0.549*	0.011	–0.129	1.523***
	(0.239)	(0.242)	(0.257)	(0.226)
N	4,000	4,000	4,000	3,998
Groups	16	16	16	16
Observations per group	250.0	250.0	250.0	249.9

Notes: Dependent variable is TV share in the socio-demographic groups. Method is generalized estimating equation (GEE) assuming a linear combination of the covariates, specifying a square root transformation of the dependent variable and an independent within-group correlation. a. Reference category is 'Friendlies'. b. Reference category is West Germany. c. Reference category is '1995'. d. Reference category is 'Away match'. e. Reference category is special interest or regional network. f. Reference category is workdays (Monday to Friday). g. Reference category is all other time slots. h. Reference category is 'Spring'. i. Reference category is 'Below 0°C'. j. Reference category is 'No rain at all'. * < 0.05; ** < 0.01; *** < 0.001.

Table 4.3 TV ratings for matches of the women's national soccer team from 2003 to 2017

Independent variables	Model 5	Model 6	Model 7	Model 8
	Younger women	Older women	Younger men	Older men
Athletic relevance[a]				
Qualification	0.548***	0.275***	0.381***	0.431***
	(0.100)	(0.074)	(0.099)	(0.072)
Olympic Group	1.690***	1.703***	2.290***	1.963***
	(0.134)	(0.103)	(0.137)	(0.104)
Olympic Final	2.140***	1.842***	2.586***	1.814***
	(0.124)	(0.097)	(0.129)	(0.099)
EURO Group	−0.373**	0.124	−0.023	0.655***
	(0.136)	(0.109)	(0.141)	(0.104)
EURO Final	1.302***	1.442***	1.595***	1.604***
	(0.123)	(0.103)	(0.127)	(0.102)
World Group	3.021***	1.952***	2.790***	2.293***
	(0.117)	(0.093)	(0.119)	(0.093)
World Final	3.566***	2.691***	3.431***	2.759***
	(0.132)	(0.100)	(0.131)	(0.101)
Opponent[b]				
Medium	0.536***	0.435***	0.380***	0.213***
	(0.068)	(0.054)	(0.070)	(0.053)
Low	0.327***	0.272***	0.333***	0.025
	(0.083)	(0.069)	(0.086)	(0.069)
East[c]	−0.984**	−1.445***	−1.449***	−1.128**
	(0.350)	(0.339)	(0.376)	(0.326)
Year[d]				
2004	0.043	−0.070	−0.459*	0.056
	(0.228)	(0.187)	(0.228)	(0.194)
2005	−0.134	−0.276	−0.655*	−0.159
	(0.259)	(0.207)	(0.253)	(0.208)
2006	−0.227	−0.411*	−0.778**	−0.321
	(0.249)	(0.199)	(0.244)	(0.202)
2007	−0.670**	−0.434*	−1.163***	−0.379*
	(0.197)	(0.175)	(0.206)	(0.184)
2008	0.050	0.328	−0.300	0.267
	(0.229)	(0.186)	(0.228)	(0.195)
2009	0.251	−0.029	−0.381	0.066
	(0.223)	(0.185)	(0.224)	(0.192)
2010	0.476	−0.127	−0.539	−0.292
	(0.274)	(0.221)	(0.286)	(0.226)
2011	0.388	0.147	−0.246	0.134
	(0.209)	(0.182)	(0.214)	(0.190)
2012	0.747**	0.181	0.126	0.067
	(0.222)	(0.190)	(0.223)	(0.197)

(*continued*)

Table 4.3 (Cont.)

Independent variables	Model 5	Model 6	Model 7	Model 8
	Younger women	*Older women*	*Younger men*	*Older men*
2013	0.394	−0.154	−0.248	−0.060
	(0.213)	(0.181)	(0.213)	(0.188)
2014	−0.578	−0.714**	−1.611***	−0.907***
	(0.309)	(0.214)	(0.308)	(0.215)
2015	−1.274***	−0.584**	−1.315***	−0.773***
	(0.208)	(0.177)	(0.211)	(0.186)
2016	−0.082	−0.687***	−1.591***	−0.979***
	(0.229)	(0.191)	(0.239)	(0.199)
2017	0.437	−0.104	−0.635*	−0.432*
	(0.236)	(0.200)	(0.245)	(0.209)
East * Year				
2004	0.635	0.437	0.691	0.098
	(0.386)	(0.368)	(0.413)	(0.352)
2005	0.554	0.631	0.848	0.388
	(0.478)	(0.423)	(0.488)	(0.387)
2006	0.318	0.852*	0.866	0.169
	(0.487)	(0.396)	(0.468)	(0.377)
2007	−0.206	0.614	0.636	0.144
	(0.397)	(0.365)	(0.415)	(0.351)
2008	−0.272	0.472	0.737	−0.049
	(0.407)	(0.361)	(0.407)	(0.350)
2009	0.603	0.367	0.845*	−0.009
	(0.399)	(0.373)	(0.422)	(0.354)
2010	0.673	0.916*	1.189*	0.416
	(0.504)	(0.437)	(0.533)	(0.424)
2011	−0.054	0.476	0.484	0.367
	(0.371)	(0.361)	(0.401)	(0.350)
2012	0.208	0.574	0.721	0.089
	(0.410)	(0.390)	(0.431)	(0.376)
2013	0.290	0.619	0.887*	0.201
	(0.376)	(0.362)	(0.399)	(0.347)
2014	0.674	1.062*	0.874	0.188
	(0.600)	(0.427)	(0.653)	(0.416)
2015	0.525	0.957**	0.475	0.484
	(0.385)	(0.362)	(0.418)	(0.352)
2016	0.607	0.953*	0.491	0.543
	(0.382)	(0.369)	(0.439)	(0.360)
2017	0.315	0.802*	0.781	0.188
	(0.420)	(0.389)	(0.455)	(0.384)
Home[e]	0.031	0.162**	0.118	0.224***
	(0.072)	(0.053)	(0.070)	(0.051)
Major[f]	0.825***	1.592***	1.195***	1.982***
	(0.139)	(0.115)	(0.138)	(0.100)

Table 4.3 (Cont.)

Independent variables	Model 5	Model 6	Model 7	Model 8
	Younger women	*Older women*	*Younger men*	*Older men*
Weekend[g]	0.385***	0.320***	0.130*	–0.008
	(0.057)	(0.046)	(0.061)	(0.046)
Prime Time[h]	1.258***	0.756***	1.663***	0.579***
	(0.073)	(0.067)	(0.078)	(0.067)
Season[i]				
Spring	0.431***	0.208**	0.101	0.045
	(0.110)	(0.076)	(0.106)	(0.073)
Summer	–0.100	–0.046	0.005	0.022
	(0.088)	(0.061)	(0.084)	(0.057)
Winter	–0.146	0.069	–0.331	–0.101
	(0.182)	(0.126)	(0.182)	(0.123)
Temperature[j]				
Low	–0.656***	–0.485**	–0.762***	–0.346**
	(0.167)	(0.140)	(0.167)	(0.130)
Warm	–0.711***	–0.425**	–0.754***	–0.277
	(0.172)	(0.141)	(0.171)	(0.133)
Very warm	–0.617**	–0.458**	–0.580**	–0.182
	(0.179)	(0.148)	(0.179)	(0.139)
Rain[k]				
Slight	0.230*	0.102	0.206*	0.186*
	(0.101)	(0.081)	(0.104)	(0.079)
Moderate	0.260*	0.019	0.023	0.182
	(0.112)	(0.097)	(0.121)	(0.094)
Strong	–0.688	–0.029	–0.069	–0.101
	(0.337)	(0.227)	(0.297)	(0.237)
Constant	1.100***	2.035***	2.548***	3.379***
	(0.256)	(0.224)	(0.257)	(0.222)
N	3,008	3,008	3,008	3,007
Groups	16	16	16	16
Observations per group	188.0	188.0	188.0	187.9

Notes: Dependent variable is TV share in the socio-demographic groups. Method is generalized estimating equation (GEE) assuming a linear combination of the covariates, specifying a square root transformation of the dependent variable and an independent within-group correlation. a. Reference category is 'Friendlies'. b. Reference category is 'Top', that is, opponent teams occupying FIFA ranks 1 to 5. c. Reference category is West Germany. d. Reference category is '2003'. e. Reference category is 'Away match'. f. Reference category is special interest or regional network. g. Reference category is workdays (Monday to Friday). h. Reference category is all other time slots. i. Reference category is 'Spring'. j. Reference category is 'Below 0°C'. k. Reference category is 'No rain at all'. $* < 0.05; ** < 0.01; *** < 0.001$.

Furthermore, the multivariate analyses support the impression that 2011 marked the peak of public interest in women's soccer. Since the 2011 'home' World Cup, the TV ratings among the different socio-demographic groups seemed to be characterized by different trends. However, a common finding across all socio-demographic groups is that there is an increase in ratings in 2017. When the models for the entire period (Models 1 to 4) are compared with the models for the period since 2003 (Models 5 to 8), the coefficients for the year dummies make it evident that there has been no significant trend toward increased ratings since 2003. Accordingly, it can be summarized that the popularity of the women's national soccer team has significantly increased since the mid-1990s but that the ratings are now stagnating.

The multivariate analyses confirm again the existence of persistent legacies of the German divide. Across all socio-demographic groups, TV ratings for the women's national soccer team are significantly lower in East Germany. Even though the visual depiction of the predictive margins estimated for all models seems to suggest that the audience share gap between West and East German TV ratings could have decreased since 2011 (Figures 4.3 and 4.4), these trends are not statistically

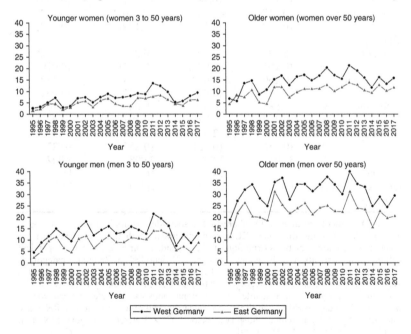

Figure 4.3 TV ratings for matches of the women's national soccer team from 1995 to 2017

Note: Predictive margins estimated on the basis of Models 1 to 4.

Popularity of women's national soccer 89

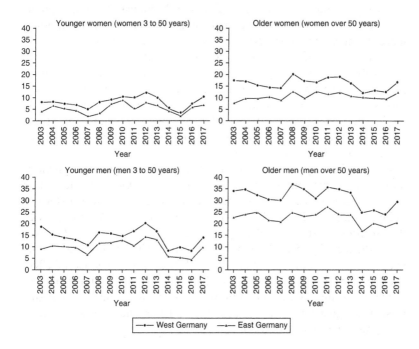

Figure 4.4 TV ratings for matches of the women's national soccer team from 2003 to 2017

Note: Predictive margins estimated on the basis of Models 5 to 8.

significant. More precisely, the models estimated for the entire period show only some significant interaction effects between *East* and the year dummies for 'Younger women'. Hence, significant evidence for convergence in audience behavior is only found for the socio-demographic group with the lowest interest in women's soccer (Model 1). However, the models estimated for the period from 2003 to 2017 provide support for the idea that some significant convergence might also exist for 'Older women' and for 'Younger men' (Models 6 and 7). In contrast, persistent divergence of consumption patterns seems to be characteristically for 'Older men' (Models 4 and 8).

Concerning match characteristics, all socio-demographic groups prefer, not surprisingly, matches that are more relevant. Thus, World Cup and Olympic soccer tournament finals attract the largest audiences. German TV audiences show an ambiguous stance toward the quality of the opponent team and, by implication, toward match outcome uncertainty. German TV audiences seem to have a preference for fixtures

90 *Popularity of women's national soccer*

involving medium-quality teams. Echoing Szymanski (2003), it might be concluded that viewers prefer matches in which the women's national soccer team enjoys some advantage but which are not too one-sided.

Furthermore, the analyses provide substantial evidence for the claim that visibility, accessibility, and opportunity costs matter for consumers. In other words: The women's national soccer team reaches larger audience shares when its matches are telecast by one of the major public service networks. Hence, Chancellor Schröder's demand that these networks should broadcast more women's soccer has probably benefitted the popularity of women's soccer.

Concerning opportunity costs, the analyses support previous findings on sports entertainment consumption in Germany according to which telecasts during prime time attract larger audiences (Meier & Leinwather, 2012, 2013; Meier, Strauß, & Riedl, 2017). Moreover, with the exception of the socio-demographic group of 'Older men', German TV audiences significantly prefer weekend matches. In contrast, home matches increase only the demand of older audiences. A seasonal effect could only be detected for female audiences who seem to prefer matches shown in spring. Weather conditions also appear to matter. Not surprisingly, higher temperatures decrease audience shares, the impact of precipitation is less clear and inconsistent.

Conclusion

The chapter has shown that the women's national soccer team has enjoyed growing popularity since the mid-1990s. However, after the public interest peaked during the 'home' World Cup of 2011, ratings now seem to have stagnated. Accordingly, the findings presented here only cautiously support the 'future of soccer is feminine' claim. Yet, the data also illustrate that women's soccer is able to reach impressive audience figures provided that the matches are visible, heavily promoted, and easily accessible. Large audiences can, in particular, be generated in the context of mega-sport events. In contrast, less relevant matches stimulate significantly smaller demand and show that women's soccer is still a niche sport.

Moreover, the findings presented here contradict the idea that younger cohorts are more prone to watching matches of the women's national soccer team. On the contrary, 'Older men' represent the most dedicated fans of the women's national soccer team as measured by TV ratings. Regarding the 'future of soccer is feminine'-claim, the results are rather sobering due to the age effects found. The fact that younger audiences are less likely to watch matches of the women's national soccer team contradicts theoretical expectations according to which women's soccer should be more popular among younger people who—in general—hold more egalitarian gender-role attitudes. Quite in contrast, older audiences—irrespective of their sex—are more likely to watch women's soccer than younger ones. These findings allows certainly for different explanations.

The lower appeal of the women's national soccer team among younger cohorts might reflect a decreasing importance for sports broadcasting for younger audiences who are confronted with a much broader range of entertainment choices than any generation before. Moreover, younger media consumers might be less likely to watch national soccer team matches due to a general decline in national identification within a generation that has been socialized in a globalized and multi-ethnic world. Besides, it is conceivable that the lower TV ratings for the women's team result from changing viewing habits, that is, the decreasing popularity of traditional linear TV in general, and of the public service broadcasters in particular, among younger audiences. As Hutchins and Rowe (2012) have emphasized, the rise of 'digital plenitude', that is, a variety of platforms and a diversity of content, will further fragmentize audiences and render the idea of a linear and general interest TV, which the PSBs best exemplified, increasingly anachronistic (Boyle, 2014). The implications are highly unfortunate for many niche sports in Europe, which traditionally relied on the coverage by the PSBs. These insights are of relevance for women's soccer because matches of the women's national soccer team have been exclusively telecast by German PSBs but not by one of the major German commercial broadcasters, such as, RTL, Sat.1 and ProSieben. These commercial channels attract, on average, a substantially younger audience than the two major PSB channels, ARD1 and ZDF. In contrast, audience availability is much higher for the older audiences typical for the PSBs (e.g., Zubayr & Gerhard, 2005, 2011, 2017). Accordingly, the higher ratings for the women's national soccer team among older audiences might represent an audience availability or TV channel effect and reflect fading viewing habits. Older audiences are more likely to watch the PSBs and are less likely to switch channels. In any case, the implications for the future popularity of women's soccer are rather unfortunate. On the one hand, the fact that commercial broadcasters do not telecast women's soccer matches indicates that they do not perceive much commercial potential in the sport. On the other hand, the fact that younger TV audiences are less likely to be exposed to women's soccer makes it unlikely that they will develop relevant consumer capital and viewing habits (see, in general, Stigler & Becker, 1977). Sport economists have

92 *Popularity of women's national soccer*

stressed that exposure by the mass media is highly important for sports in order to attract new audiences and to create potential network externalities (Solberg, 2002). By implication, if TV ratings for the women's national soccer team are strongly dependent on accessibility and audience availability, the DFB will have to find ways to adapt to the viewing habits of younger cohorts in a multiplatform media environment in order to avoid decreasing ratings.

Concerning policy legacies, the chapter provides further evidence for lasting legacies of the German divide. East Germans are significantly less interested in the women's national soccer team and there is only limited evidence for a convergence of consumption behavior. Apparently, the marginalization of women's soccer in East German sports policies has served to create strong policy feedback on the public perception of the sport. It might be inferred that East Germans are still less willing to consider women's soccer as a serious elite sport worthy of their attention. Given the fact that girls' and women's grass-roots and elite soccer face a difficult stance in East Germany, prospects for increasing popularity for the women's national soccer team in East Germany appear to be rather bleak.

Finally, the findings once more provide evidence for the claim that women do not watch women's sport (Whiteside & Hardin, 2011). In general, numerically and proportionally more men than women watch televised sport (Gantz & Wenner, 1991; Gantz et al., 2006). This applies also to Germany where increased female TV watching has served to widen the gender gap in the consumption of sports broadcasting (Meier & Leinwather, 2012; Meier, Strauß, & Riedl, 2017). These gender differences in sport spectatorship and fan motivation are probably products of 'sex-discriminatory acculturation processes' (Sloan, 1989: 176). Hence, previous scholarship has argued that men are more involved fans (Gantz, 1981; Gantz & Wenner, 1991) because being a sports fan has been found to be an important part of male identity but not female identity (Gantz & Wenner, 1995; Dietz-Uhler et al., 2000; James & Ridinger, 2002). Moreover, women have not only been found to be less likely to watch sport, but also likely to watch sport for different reasons. A considerable share of female TV sport consumption seems to be motivated by the desire to spend quality time with partners, particularly so as men have traditionally dominated domestic entertainment choices (Gantz & Wenner, 1991). Accordingly, women might perceive such sport consumption not as leisure time but 'emotional work', that is, an activity intended to enhance others' emotional well-being. For this reason—and due to a lack of leisure time resulting from an unequal distribution of household chores—women might not choose to watch women's sport and female athletes (Whiteside & Hardin, 2011). Yet, it is important to qualify these findings. More recent research has detected a trend toward a 'feminization' of sports audiences and fans, which appears to be related to changes in gender-role orientations (Meier, Strauß, & Riedl, 2017). According to these findings, less restrictive gender-role socialization encourages female sports consumption and fandom.

Hence, another explanation is that women might simply be drawn to what is still the standard of sports, that is, men's sports (Meier & Leinwather, 2012). The sport media complex is still characterized by a strong gender bias in coverage and commentaries. This bias partly reflects hegemonic masculinity, that is, deliberate efforts to maintain male power and privilege, sexism, or heterosexism (Fink, 2015). In addition, sports entertainment is mainly produced by men for the (anticipated) preferences of a predominantly male audience (Rulofs & Hartmann-Tews, 2011; Schaaf, 2014). Furthermore, the highly instructive qualitative study conducted by Whiteside and Hardin (2011) suggested that women do not watch female athletes because of the 'shocking difference' between the mediated images of strong women engaged in an activity culturally marked as masculine and the women's everyday sense of self.

Based on the data analyzed here, it is not possible to provide a definitive answer as to which explanation is most valid. In any case, it is important to reflect on the fact that younger women who grew up in a more gender-equal society, and should be more confident in their entertainment choices, are substantially less likely to follow matches of the women's national soccer team. The maximum ratings achieved in this particular socio-demographic group are substantially lower than the maximum ratings in any other group. Accordingly, the gender gap in the consumption of women's sport might rather increase than decrease. The persistent disinterest of women in women's soccer represents a substantial challenge for the future popularity of the sport.

In sum, the chapter has shown that the women's national soccer team has successfully occupied its niche in German TV sports consumption. The team is able to attract impressive audiences in the context of mega-sport events. Nevertheless, the chapter provides little evidence for the idea that the future of soccer consumption will become more female. TV ratings have not shown a growth trend since the 'home' World Cup of 2011. Moreover, the team is substantially less popular in East Germany, among younger audiences and women. Thus, the DFB faces serious challenges in maintaining the current popularity of the team.

Notes

1 Herzog (2018) suggests that the West German press was divided in its depiction of women's soccer. Interestingly, the tabloid *Bild* and the rather conservative quality newspaper, *Frankfurter Allgemeine Zeitung*, were supportive of women's soccer.
2 There is no doubt that women's soccer has attracted lesbian women and served as a haven where being different was accepted (Herzog, 2018: 67).

5 How feminine will the future of soccer be?

Introduction

This book has started from the insight that the development of women's soccer is strongly related to progress toward more gender equality. Nations characterized by high levels of gender inequality are more likely to field no national women's soccer team at all, whereas national teams from more gender-equal societies tend to perform better in international women's soccer. Hence it appears Sepp Blatter's claim that the 'future of soccer is feminine' could be valid if societies actually progress toward more gender equality and if there is a linear relationship between macro-social gender equality and the development of women's soccer.

These basic insights represent the main rationale for choosing Germany as a case study on women's soccer. Germany is one of the most gender-equal societies in the world and, notwithstanding legacies of social conservatism, continues to be characterized by a secular trend toward more gender equality. Female labor force participation continues to increase and gender-role attitudes have modernized (Trappe et al., 2015; Pollmann-Schult & Reynolds, 2017). Moreover, Germany has been one of the most successful nations in women's soccer. Accordingly, with regard to Sepp Blatter's claim, Germany should illustrate how feminine the future of soccer might actually be. An additional rationale for studying the development of women's soccer in Germany has been that reunified Germany allows for elaborating on the impact of different policy legacies (Konietzka & Kreyenfeld, 2002; Bauernschuster & Rainer, 2011; Hanel & Riphan, 2011).

The preceding chapters have examined the development and state of women's soccer in Germany in three key domains: grass-roots girls' and women's soccer (Chapter 2), the women's national soccer league (Chapter 3), and the popularity of the women's national team

96 *How feminine will the future of soccer be?*

(Chapter 4). The findings will be first discussed with regard to the key question of whether the future of soccer will be more female. Then, the impact of policy legacies will be theorized as well as the options for soccer bodies to promote girls' and women's soccer.

Toward an ever more female future for soccer?

Concerning a (more) female future for soccer, the empirical studies leave an ambiguous impression. First, the analyses demonstrate that soccer has become more female in a number of respects. An impressive number of girls' and women's teams is participating in grass-roots soccer, attendance for league soccer has increased, German women's soccer teams compete successfully in international club competitions, and the women's national soccer team is able to draw impressive audiences. Concerning trends, the number of grass-roots teams has increased by 25 percent within a decade, attendance in first-tier women's league soccer has almost quadrupled over a 20-year period and audience figures for the women's national soccer team have been growing by 4 percent per year over a 23-year period.

However, these findings on positive trends have to be qualified. Most problematic is that all studies indicate that women's soccer seems to face problems of growth. The number of grass-roots teams, the average attendance for first-tier league matches, and TV ratings all have been declining recently. It would be an exaggeration to diagnose this as a crisis of women's soccer in Germany. However, the rich empirical evidence presented here strongly suggests that there is no linear trend toward a growth in women's soccer.

Therefore, with regard to the relationship between macro-social gender equality and the development of women's soccer, the findings presented here suggest that the erosion of traditional gender hierarchies at the macro level creates opportunities for female participation in traditionally male sports, and for women's sport to be a legitimate form of sports entertainment. However, the secular trend toward more gender equality within German society does not translate linearly into self-reinforcing growth for women's soccer.

The predominantly macro-social design of the studies conducted provides only tentative suggestions around which factors may account for stagnation in the development of women's soccer. Socio-economic and demographic trends might work against further growth in girls' and women's soccer but their impact remains unclear (see 'Practical implications, below). Moreover, the analyses defy the idea that a more gender-equal socialization results in a more positive attitude toward

How feminine will the future of soccer be? 97

women's soccer as sports entertainment. Quite the contrary, younger women, who have been socialized into a much more gender-equal society, show the lowest amount of interest in women's soccer as sports entertainment. Whereas several factors might account for this finding, female disinterest in women's sport represents a more general pattern in Germany.[1]

These open questions and counterintuitive results make the limitations of a predominantly macro-social account evident. Macro-social factors do not influence the development of girls' and women's soccer in a deterministic manner. Hence, as Susan Lagaert and Henk Roose (2018: 546) have correctly emphasized, a macro-social perspective

> needs to be complemented with qualitative and quantitative research on how meso-level institutions, such as sports federations and sports clubs, families, the media, schools and peer groups function as gatekeepers and mediate or moderate the effect of macro-level gender equality.

Thus, in order to address the question of which factors work against future growth in girls' and women's soccer, multilevel theoretical and empirical research is necessary to trace how macro-level gender equality and more gender-equal socialization in a distinct institutional setting relates to individual attitudes and behavior at the micro-level. The results presented here suggest that the future of soccer might indeed be more female. However, progress proceeds rather slowly and cannot be taken for granted. There are good reasons to assume that further efforts by the DFB and its state associations are necessary in order to promote future growth. Here, the insights into the relevance of institutional legacies, which the studies have yielded, are of utmost importance.

The impact of institutional legacies

Reunified Germany represents an ideal comparative case study for examining the impact of contrasting institutional legacies on the development of women's soccer. In both Germanys, there existed a tension between general and sector specific gender regimes. Whereas capitalist West Germany represented the more gender unequal society in general, since the 1970s, gender discrimination in soccer has gradually dissipated. In contrast, the more gender-equal communist East Germany marginalized women's soccer until the collapse of the regime.

Taken together, the chapters suggest that sector-specific gender discrimination has been more decisive for the development of women's

98 *How feminine will the future of soccer be?*

soccer than general gender inequality. East Germany continues to lag behind with regard to the development of grass-roots girls' and women's soccer, and to the popularity of the women's national soccer team. Hence, higher gender equality in East Germany did not translate into participation in women's soccer, nor in interest in the sport as entertainment. The lasting impact of gender discrimination in East German soccer is theoretically remarkable because this discrimination was not motivated by attempts to preserve male hegemony but by purely utilitarian calculations about athletic success. Women's soccer was marginalized because it was viewed as irrelevant for the Olympic medal record.

Nevertheless, the strictly utilitarian discrimination came with lasting resource and interpretive effects. Due to a denial of public subsidies, women's soccer would not have developed in East Germany at all if not for some enthusiasts in a few company sports organizations. Moreover, the sport remained not only under-resourced until reunification but was also denied recognition as a serious competitive or even an elite sport. Thus, communist sports policies illustrate Williams' (2003: 8) conclusion that women's soccer's access to any kind of equality is hampered by structures that reinforce female soccer as primarily an amateur and voluntary leisure activity. In contrast, girls' and women's soccer development improved greatly in West Germany after the soccer association had abandoned its hostile stance. Since the 1980s, women's soccer has gained huge benefits from being embedded into the association's professional structures. Thus, both the number of grass-roots teams and the public appeal of the national team are substantially higher in West Germany. Hence, the German case illustrates that, even though general gender inequality is relevant for the development of women's soccer, meso-level institutions are decisive in mediating general gender inequality. Accordingly, the results presented in the chapters might give some—albeit limited—hints as to how girls' and women's soccer can be promoted. Yet, it is also important to realize that the persistent East–West lag in the development of girls' and women's soccer in Germany illustrates how difficult it is to overcome policy legacies.

Practical implications

Although research presented in this book has adopted a strictly quantitative and macro-social perspective, the empirical analyses come with practical implications because they defy simple deterministic ideas. The studies demonstrate that policy legacies and macro-social contexts matter for the development of girls' and women's soccer. However, these factors cannot account for the substantial regional variety in team density found in Germany. As discussed in Chapter 2, the state associations of Lower Saxony and Bavaria, which cover large and diverse territories, demonstrate that girls' and women's soccer can develop under quite different economic and socio-demographic conditions. The analyses further indicate that a club's commitment to girls' and women's soccer is important for the development of the sports. Hence, it appears that unfavorable contextual factors, in particular rural restructuring and female outmigration, might serve as barriers for the development of girls' and women's soccer but that there is still substantial discretion for soccer organizations.

These conclusions concerning the key role of sports organizations are further supported by the lasting policy legacies of the German divide. In East Germany, policymakers decided to focus on elite sports that promised a high return on investment in terms of medals. However, grass-roots sports in general, and female sports needs in particular, were given a low priority. The outcome was a tremendously successful elite sports system but low participation in popular sports, in particular among girls and women. In contrast, the more supportive approach adopted by the West German soccer association inspired female mass participation in soccer and served to create one of the most successful national teams.

Moreover, the analyses allow for some conclusions to be drawn on policies that are likely to promote public attention for women's soccer. The findings presented here suggest that marketing strategies can actually increase public attention for women's soccer. Hence, the 'home' World Cup has increased TV audiences as well as stadium attendance in first-tier league soccer. However, the results indicate that sustaining such effects might be difficult. Furthermore, improving the accessibility and visibility of women's soccer by forcing the major public service broadcasters to televise the matches of the national team has served to increase TV ratings. As demonstrated, these general interest networks represent a highly attractive platform for the women's national team, resulting in impressive TV ratings. Unfortunately, it is not quite clear whether these high audience figures will be sustainable under conditions of 'digital plenitude' (Hutchins & Rowe, 2012) as the very audience habits, which account for the impressive ratings, are fading. As with other niche sports, women's soccer is likely to face substantial challenges when it comes to preserving the public's interest in a multi-platform media environment characterized by increased audience fragmentation. The women's national soccer team will have to deal with the

100 *How feminine will the future of soccer be?*

dilemma between keeping loyal audiences and a more diversified media strategy, which aims to address the younger audience.

Concerning the attendance levels of first-tier women's league soccer, the analyses have evidenced that the growing engagement of major clubs, which field successful men's teams, is likely to increase attendance. It is likely the women's first-tier soccer teams would benefit from the more professional infrastructure these clubs have at their disposal, as well as from the fact that these clubs represent established brands. Moreover, only major soccer clubs can provide the subsidies needed to meet the increasing professional needs that result, among others, from more intensified European competition. At present it seems that women's first-tier soccer seems hardly sustainable as sports entertainment without such subsidies. However, the growth in attendance generated by the involvement of major soccer clubs comes with more volatility. Nevertheless, the DFB might consider encouraging the trend toward major clubs even though it means that pioneers of women's soccer will disappear. Such a strategy implies, however, that soccer officials, women's soccer activists, and players alike share the conviction that professionalization is the key to further progress of the sport (Williams, 2003: 148). Other visions for the future of girls' and women's soccer are, however, conceivable.

In any case, in terms of practical implications, the findings presented in this book suggest that the decisions and organizational priorities of soccer associations and clubs, sports ministries, educational institutions, municipalities, and TV networks are likely to have a decisive and long-lasting impact on the development of girls' and women's soccer. Resource and interpretive effects outlive the original policies and might not be easily reversed.

Directions for future research

The book has adopted a strict quantitative approach in analyzing process-generated data. This approach has generated valid insights on the state, the development and the trajectories of girls' and women's soccer in reunified Germany. On the one hand, the findings show that soccer has indeed become more female. On the other hand, the results are likely to dampen excessive optimism regarding the growth and popularity of women's soccer. Finally, the analyses indicate that the future of women's soccer can be influenced by policy and management decisions at different levels.

However, in order to provide more valid insights into the influence of association policies, it would have been helpful to include detailed

How feminine will the future of soccer be? 101

indicators on promotional policies for girls' and women's soccer as Jacobs (2014) did in her evaluation on FIFA programs. However, without downplaying the need for strict quantitative studies, the analyses also indicate the shortcomings of a purely quantitative approach, using process-generated data. In order to provide decision makers in sport administrations, sports associations, and clubs with more specific policy advice, detailed multilevel policy and management studies are necessary. Hence, the book echoes the conclusion of the integrative review conducted by Valenti et al. (2018), that the development of girls' and women's soccer has to be studied from managerial and business perspectives. In light of the findings presented here, it seems that what would be needed are case studies on the very soccer associations and soccer clubs that are most successful in inspiring female grass-roots participation, even under rather unfavorable economic and demographic conditions. In addition, detailed studies on first-tier women's soccer clubs could bring about new insights into the preconditions needed for team success and appeal. Moreover, fine-grained multilevel studies on attitudes toward women's soccer as a sports activity and sports entertainment are necessary in order to understand how gender-role attitudes and interest in women's soccer are related in Germany.

Summary

Since 1955, when the West German soccer association forbade its member clubs to support women's soccer teams, German soccer has become substantially more female. A considerable number of grass-roots teams exist, a semi-professional league has been established, and the national team has been extremely successful on the pitch and among audiences. However, the German data indicate that there is no linear progress toward an ever-more female future for soccer, since recently the development of girls' and women's soccer has entered a phase of stagnation. After the recent performances of the women's national soccer team, which have been perceived as disappointing, some observers even speak of a crisis of girls' and women's soccer in Germany (Meuren, 2018, 2019).

Although the book has found evidence of stagnation in women's soccer in Germany, the recent trends should not be misinterpreted as indicating that the sport has reached its peak. Quite the contrary, given considerable regional diversity and variation over time, the findings presented here suggest that the future of girls' and women's soccer depends on priorities adopted by soccer organizations and other key stakeholders. However, if specific policy advice is to be provided, then more fine-grained policy and management studies are necessary.

Note

1 For example, female audiences are substantially and significantly less interested than male audiences in women's tennis (Konjer et al., 2017) or women's boxing (Stroth, 2018).

Appendix
Data and research designs

This appendix provides more detailed information on the datasets analyzed in the chapters of this book as well as on the statistical designs employed. The appendix is organized on the basis of the individual chapters.

Chapter 1

Data sources

Data on the rankings of women's national soccer teams were retrieved from the official website of the world soccer association, that is, the Fédération Internationale de Football Association (FIFA) (www.fifa.com). For measuring gender inequality, the chapter uses the Gender Inequality Value (GIV) as conducted by the United Nations Educational, Scientific and Cultural Organization (UNESCO). The GIV considers the dimensions of reproductive health, empowerment, and the labor market and ranges from '0'—perfect gender equality—to '1'—total gender inequality (for more detail, see UNESCO, 2011). Data on gross domestic product (GDP) per capita and national population were retrieved from the Human Development Reports website (UNDP, 2018) (see Table A.1). These data sources were combined in order to create a panel dataset.

Analytic strategy

Since FIFA rankings serve as a dependent variable, ordinal logistic panel regressions were performed using the xtologit command in Stata. In order to avoid many interesting between-country variations being thrown away, random effect models were calculated.

104   *Appendix*

Table A.1 Dataset on women's national soccer team performances from 2010 to 2015

Variable	N	Mean	SD	Minimum	Maximum
FIFA rank of national team[a]	1,555	63.775	36.781	1	140
Gender inequality value[b]	1,161	0.385	0.191	0.040	0.818
GDP per capita in 1,000 USD[c]	3,045	15.548	18.225	0.423	141.947
Country share of world population[c]	1,164	0.511	1.935	0	19.442

Notes: The dataset covers the period from 2010 to 2015. a. FIFA rankings as provided by FIFA's official website. b. Gender inequality index as provided by the United Nations Educational, Scientific and Cultural Organization (UNESCO). c. Data on GDP per capita and population were retrieved from the Human Development Reports website (UNDP, 2018).

Chapter 2

Data sources

The chapter relies on two different data sources, that is, (a) team data provided by the DFB, and (b) context data as conducted by official municipality statistics. These data sources have been combined using the official German municipality code (Amtlicher Gemeindeschlüssel— AGS). The AGS identifies politically independent municipalities that represent the lowest political and administrative level of Germany's federal state, for which detailed demographic and economic indicators are available.

The DFB team data

The team data provided by the DFB represent an extract of the team database administered by the DFB-Medien GmbH & Co. KG, which manages a number of databases for the DFB and its state associations. The team database includes information on all girls' and women's teams participating in a competition organized under the auspices of the DFB. The dataset analyzed here focuses on grass-roots football. The fourth tier of competitive women's football represents the highest league level analyzed here.

The basic unit of observation for the DFB team data is the 'team season', that is, an observation on an individual soccer team in a distinct season. Accordingly, the DFB data are based on 'natural' observation periods as defined by the social field. The original data covered the seasons from 2001/2002 to 2015/2016. Yet, it had to be taken into account that data sampling at the beginning of this period was not completely reliable because not all state associations were immediately able to handle the data management after the new database system had been introduced. Therefore, the datasets were restricted to the period between the seasons 2005/2006 to 2015/2016. Moreover, the original dataset included 95,891 observations for league and cup competitions. Only the former are relevant for tracing team development. Accordingly, 10,280 data points for cup competitions were removed from the DFB data, which resulted in 85,611 'team seasons'. A detailed scrutiny revealed 41 double entries in total, which were also removed. Furthermore, 1,333 units of team season data lacked information on team performance, such as, league positions, goals and points, and were, therefore, considered not to be valid. Thus, the adjusted data consists of 84,237 records on 'team seasons'. The DFB data included information on the name of the team's club, the club's postal code, which allowed for identifying the AGS, the season the team played, the state association to which the team belonged, the age class in which the team played, the division, and the seasonal outcome, measured in league positions, goals, and points.

Context data as provided by municipality statistics

The context data were retrieved from the statistical offices of the federal states, which conduct economic and demographic indicators for politically independent municipalities. The basic unit of observation is the 'municipality year' as statistical indicators are provided per municipality on an annual basis. Unfortunately, these data suffer from a number of limitations (see Meier, Konjer, & Nagm, 2017). These limitations had the effect that extensive consistency checks and re-codings were necessary and advanced statistical analyses were primarily conducted for the period after 2011.

- **Different 'statistical resolution'**: The 'statistical resolution' is much higher for smaller municipalities than for larger municipalities, in particular for the 'city-states' Berlin, Bremen, and Hamburg, which are both municipalities and federal states, but also for a substantial number of municipalities that enjoy county-level status. Therefore, the 'city-states' had to be excluded from the multivariate analyses.

106   *Appendix*

- **Different sets of statistical indicators**: The set of available statistical indicators differs across federal states. Some federal states seem to have cut the budgets of their statistical offices with the effect that the set of statistical indicators has been reduced. In particular, data for Saxony-Anhalt were incomplete and inconsistent. Therefore, the state association was not included in the multivariate analyses.
- **Temporal inconsistency of methods**: The methods for conducting certain statistical indicators are not consistent over time. For the present study, of particular relevance was that official population figures in Germany had been heavily revised by the 2011 census. The census revealed substantial measurement errors and corrected Germany's total population figure by -1.9 percent (Statistisches Bundesamt, 2013). Since previous measurement errors were correlated with municipality size and population composition, the revision of statistical procedures made it impossible to construct longitudinal population data for the period before 2011 (Christensen et al., 2015).
- **Inconsistent units of observation**: Finally, the units of observation are not always consistent since a number of municipality reforms resulted in the merger of formerly independent municipalities.

The datasets constructed

The count dataset on teams per municipality

The first dataset has been constructed to study the organizational population of girls' and women's soccer teams by counting the *Number of adult teams per municipality* and the *Number of girls' teams per municipality*, referring to all U18 teams. Accordingly, the dataset has panel character because it consists of repeated observations (team numbers) on individual units (municipalities) over time. As described above, due to inconsistencies in the statistics provided by the federal states, the dataset covers only the four-year period from the 2011/2012 to the 2015/2016 season. Both team number variables represent counts, which can only assume non-negative (or only positive) integer values. Moreover, both count variables are characterized by over-dispersion due to a substantial number of zeroes. Hence, many German municipalities host no women or girl soccer teams at all.

The dataset includes a number of context variables, mainly derived from official municipality statistics. The dummy variable *East* refers to the East German federal states and serves primarily as a proxy for institutional legacies. *County* represents a dummy variable for municipalities, which enjoy also county status. With some reservations, the variable might be considered as a rough proxy for urbanity as such municipalities with county status represent either big cities or regional centers. *Inhabitants* refers to the total number of inhabitants divided by 1,000 residing in a municipality. *Density* measures local population density as inhabitants by square kilometer. As *Inhabitants* as well as *Density* are strongly right-skewed, they have been log-transformed (*lnInhabitants* and *lnDensity*). *Youth* represents the population share of municipality inhabitants younger than 15 years and *Age* the population share of municipality inhabitants older than 65 years. *Women* refers to the share of female inhabitants in a municipality. Demographic trends have been measured by *Relative Population Change*. The indicator in year i for municipality j is defined as follows:

$$Relative\,Population\,Change_{i,j} = \frac{Inhabitants_{i,j} - \overline{Inhabitants_j}}{\overline{Inhabitants_j}} \times 100 \quad (A.1)$$

In order to compensate for the lack of GDP data at the municipality level, the *Social insured share* serves as a proxy for local employment conditions. The measure reflects the share of municipality inhabitants, which—in contrast to low wage employees—enjoy social insurance in Germany. In total, the dataset includes information on the number of women and youngster teams for 9,473 municipalities over a four-year period, equaling 37,892 observations in total (Table A.2).

The dataset on team survival

The second dataset represents a dataset on team survival in which time-to-event, that is, time-to-team dissolution, serves as the dependent variable. The analyses are restricted to the period from the season 2005/2006 to 2015/2016. Accordingly, the data were left-truncated or left-censored. More precisely, for all teams that were established before the 2005/2006 season, the actual date of founding is treated as unknown. Right-censoring occurs for teams which survive the 2015/2016 season.

In contrast to the count dataset, the survival dataset includes more detailed indicators on individual teams. *Teams per club* refers to the entire number of girls' and womens' team in the respective club. *Relegation* represents a dummy variable for teams, which were recently relegated. Conversely, *Promotion* represents a dummy variable for recently promoted teams. *League* indicates the rank of the league in which the team was playing. Constructing one unified indicator for

108   *Appendix*

Table A.2 The count dataset—girls' and women's soccer teams per municipality

Variables	N	Mean	SD	Min	Max
Dependent Variables					
Total teams	37,893	0.624	2.243	0	72
Adult teams	37,893	0.265	0.869	0	25
Youth teams	37,893	0.359	1.482	0	52
Local context					
East	37,893	0.214	0.410	0	1
County	37,893	0.008	0.089	0	1
Inhabitants	37,893	5.200	24.682	0.009	1,429.584
lnInhabitants	37,893	0.418	1.457	−4.711	7.265
Density	37,893	162.608	247.042	2.434	4,601.172
lnDensity	37,893	4.528	1.004	0.889	8.434
Women	37,893	50.015	1.822	21.809	64.286
Youth	37,893	13.403	2.422	0.000	30.000
Age	37,893	20.409	4.015	2.051	63.636
Social	37,893	37.049	5.169	0.000	89.655
Relative	37,893	−0.028	1.671	−23.485	15.63
Time		4.528			
Year	37,893	2013.500	1.118	2012	2015
Association					
Baden	37,893	0.015	0.120	0	1
Bavaria	37,893	0.213	0.410	0	1
Brandenburg	37,893	0.044	0.205	0	1
Hesse	37,893	0.045	0.207	0	1
Mecklenburg-West Pomerania	37,893	0.080	0.271	0	1
Middle Rhine	37,893	0.010	0.102	0	1
Lower Saxony	37,893	0.105	0.306	0	1
Rhineland	37,893	0.153	0.360	0	1
Saarland	37,893	0.005	0.074	0	1
Schleswig-Holstein	37,893	0.117	0.322	0	1
South Baden	37,893	0.032	0.175	0	1
South West Germany	37,893	0.090	0.286	0	1
Thuringia	37,893	0.090	0.286	0	1

league membership proved difficult due to the diverse league structures in the state associations (see Table A.3). *Age class* indicates the age class in which the team is playing. These data were combined with context information derived from municipality statistics (see Table A.4).

While these context variables are defined as described above, it is important to note that in the survival dataset *County* correlates moderately with *lnInhabitants* ($r = 0.709$; $p < 0.001$) as well as with *lnDensity*

Table A.3 Coding of the unified league indicator

Unified league indicator	League level denominations according to state associations
Level 1	Baden: Verbandsliga; Bavaria: Bayernliga; Berlin: Verbandsliga; Brandenburg: Landesliga; Bremen: Verbandsliga; Hamburg: Verbandsliga; Hesse: Hessenliga; Mecklenburg West Pommerenia: Verbandsliga; Middle Rhine: Verbandsliga; Lower Rhine: Niederrheinliga; Lower Saxony: Oberliga Niedersachsen; Rhineland: Rheinlandliga; Saarland: Verbandsliga; Saxony: Landesliga; Saxony-Anhalt: Verbandsliga; Schleswig-Holstein: Schleswig-Holstein-Liga; South Baden: Verbandsliga; South West: Verbandsliga; Thuringia: Verbandsliga; Westphalia: Verbandsliga; Württemberg: Verbandsliga
Level 2	Baden: Landesliga; Bavaria: Landesliga; Berlin: Landesliga; Brandenburg: Kreisliga; Bremen: Landesliga; Hamburg: Landesliga; Hesse: Verbandsliga; Mecklenburg-West Pommerenia: Kreisoberliga; Middle Rhine: Landesliga; Lower Rhine: Landesliga; Lower Saxony: Landesliga; Rhineland: Bezirksliga; Saarland: Landesliga; Saxony: Landesklasse; Saxony Anhalt: Landesliga; Schleswig-Holstein: Verbandsliga; South Baden: Landesliga; South West: Landesliga; Thuringia: Landesklasse; Westphalia: Landesliga; Württemberg: Landesliga
Level 3	Baden: Kreisliga; Bavaria: Bezirksoberliga; Berlin: Bezirksliga; Brandenburg: 1. Kreisklasse; Bremen: Bezirksliga; Hamburg: Bezirksliga; Hesse: Gruppenliga; Mecklenburg West Pommerenia: Kreisliga; Middle Rhine: Bezirksliga; Lower Rhine: Bezirksliga; Lower Saxony: Bezirksliga; Rhineland: Kreisklasse; Saarland: Bezirksliga; Saxony: Kreisoberliga; Saxony Anhalt: Regionalklasse; Schleswig-Holstein: Kreisliga; South Baden: Bezirksliga; South West: Bezirksliga (Verband); Thuringia: Kreisoberliga; Westphalia: Bezirksliga; Württemberg: Regionalliga
Level 4	Bavaria: Bezirksliga; Bremen: 1. Kreisliga/Stadtliga; Hamburg: Kreisliga; Hesse: Oberliga (Region); Mittelrhein: Kreisliga A; Lower Saxony: Kreisliga A; Lower Saxony: Kreisliga; Saarland: Bezirksklasse; Saxony: 1. Kreisliga (A); Saxony Anhalt: Kreisliga; Schleswig-Holstein: Kreisklasse A; South Baden: 1. Kreisliga (A); Thuringia: Kreisliga; Westphalia: Kreisliga A; Württemberg: Bezirksliga
Level 5	Bavaria: Kreisliga; Hamburg: Sonderliga; Hesse: A-Liga(Region); Lower Saxony: 1. Kreisklasse; Saxony: 1. Kreisklasse; Saxony Anhalt: 1. Kreisklasse; Südbaden: 2. Kreisliga (B); Westfalen: Kreisliga B; Württemberg: Kreisliga A und Kreisliga
Level 6	Bavaria: Kreisklasse; Hesse: B-Liga (Region); Lower Saxony: 2. Kreisklasse; South Baden: Kleinfeldklasse
Level 7	3. Kreisklasse

Table A.4 The survival dataset—girls' and women's soccer team dissolution

Variables	N	Mean	SD	Min	Max
Dependent variable					
Team dissolution	76,400	0.257	0.437	0	1
Local context					
East	76,400	0.037	0.189	0	1
County level status	76,400	0.120	0.325	0	1
Inhabitants	23,720	73.673	200.953	0.184	1,429.584
lnInhabitants	23,720	9.763	1.553	5.215	14.173
Density	23,720	584.401	765.434	9.176	4,601.172
lnDensity	23,720	5.711	1.145	2.217	8.434
Women share	23,720	50.858	1.092	40.677	54.800
Youth share	23,720	13.700	1.579	7.754	21.406
Social	23,720	36.441	3.461	14.043	55.861
Relative population change	23,720	−0.014	0.998	−7.740	11.965
Association					
Baden	76,400	0.038	0.192	0	1
Bavaria	76,400	0.223	0.417	0	1
Brandenburg	76,400	0.0160	0.125	0	1
Middle Rhine	76,400	0.069	0.254	0	1
Rhineland	76,400	0.044	0.204	0	1
Hesse	76,400	0.082	0.274	0	1
Mecklenburg-West Pomerania	76,400	0.007	0.081	0	1
Lower Saxony	76,400	0.324	0.468	0	1
Saarland	76,400	0.023	0.150	0	1
Schleswig-Holstein	76,400	0.065	0.247	0	1
South Baden	76,400	0.066	0.247	0	1
South West Germany	76,400	0.029	0.169	0	1
Thuringia	76,400	0.015	0.120	0	1
Club level					
Number of teams	76,400	3.192	2.120	1	19
Team level					
League	76,288	2.800	1.539	1	9
Promotion	76,400	0.117	0.321	0	1
Relegation	76,400	0.160	0.367	0	1
Age class					
Women	76,400	0.382	0.486	0	1
A Juniors	76,400	0.009	0.096	0	1
B Juniors	76,400	0.227	0.419	0	1
C Juniors	76,400	0.175	0.380	0	1
D Juniors	76,400	0.151	0.358	0	1
E Juniors	76,400	0.052	0.222	0	1
F Juniors	76,400	0.003	0.056	0	1

Appendix 111

($r = 0.619$; $p < 0.001$). Thus, county-level status of a municipality can be considered to represent a rough proxy for urbanity.

Analytic strategy

Analyzing the count dataset on team numbers per municipality requires methods for count data in order to take the limited number of possible values of the response variable into account. Due to the over-dispersion in the dataset, negative binomial regression techniques have been chosen as appropriate (Hilbe, 2014). Since the dataset has panel character, a generalized estimation equations (GEE) approach fitting population-averaged panel-data models was employed (Rabe-Hasketh & Skrondal, 2012: 560–561). In order to identify a working correlation matrix, the approach employed here followed Hardin and Hilbe (2013) who suggested using the quasi-likelihood under the independence model information criterion (QIC) as proposed by Pan (2001). The correlation matrix was identified as exchangeable.

Whereas the count dataset is treated as 'simple' panel dataset, *East* and the state associations represents additional tiers in the data structure. However, the short-term character of the panel dataset serves to limit opportunities for multilevel analysis. Accordingly, the impact of state associations was modeled by a series of dummy variables and robust standard errors. Since *Age* and *Youth* proved to be moderately correlated ($r = -0.583$; $p < 0.001$), *Age* was dropped from the analyses. Moreover, as *lnInhabitants* and *lnDensity* were strongly correlated ($r = 0.714$; $p < 0.001$), *lnInhabitants* serves as sole indicator for urbanity.

Since in the survival dataset, time-to-event, that is, time-to-team dissolution, serves as the dependent variable, semiparametric Cox-Hazard regressions were employed. Due to the fact that in the survival dataset, *County* represents a valid indicator for urbanity, models for the entire period from the 2005/2006 to the 2015/2016 season were calculated using *County* as the municipality context indicator. For the period covering the 2011/2012 to the 2015/2016 season, models including more detailed context level indicators were estimated. All models were estimated with and without the state association dummies.

Chapter 3

Data sources

Official attendance data for the one-tier Frauen-Bundesliga (FBL) are available from the 1998/1999 season. Data on home site characteristics

112 *Appendix*

have been retrieved from the statistical offices of the federal states. The weather conditions at the time of the kick-off were determined using data from the public archives of the German Meteorological Service (Deutscher Wetterdienst—DWD).

The dataset

Attendance for the home team serves as the dependent variable ($Attendance_t$). In order to account for consumer loyalty or habit persistence, the usual procedure of creating a lagged predictor, referring to the match immediately played before, was applied ($Attendance_{t-1}$; $AttendanceAwayMatch_{t-1}$) (see Borland & Lye, 1992). Moreover, the research design follows Pawlowski and Anders (2012) who calculated the average attendance for the entire previous season for the home and the away team ($MeanAttHome_{Season-1}$; $MeanAttAway_{Season-1}$) in order to derive an inter-seasonal indicator for habit persistence. Since no attendance figures for second league women's teams are available, including the indicator in the models serves to reduce the number of cases.

The approach for coding control variables follows, very much, the canonical approaches of empirical sports economics, which have demonstrated that specific quality factors determine the demand for sports entertainment. These quality features are sporting relevance, athletic quality, and uncertainty of outcome (see, for excellent reviews, Borland & MacDonald, 2003; Buraimo, 2008; García & Rodríguez, 2009).

The sporting quality of the FBL matches was measured by the league positions of the two involved teams (*HomeRank* and *AwayRank*). As the study conducted by Meier, Konjer and Leinwather (2016) on the FBL has demonstrated, due to the imbalanced character of the league, these indicators suffice as proxies for team quality. Team rankings were strongly correlated with the teams' win percentages during the last three matches and with the number of German national team players in the teams.

Concerning the uncertainty of the league, sport economists have distinguished between three distinct dimensions of uncertainty (Cairns et al., 1986), that is, inter-seasonal uncertainty, uncertainty of league outcome and uncertainty of match outcome. Given the fact that the FBL is rather imbalanced, a measure of inter-seasonal uncertainty was not included in the analyses. In order to account for uncertainty of league outcome, the approach adopted here follows Janssens and Késenne (1987), who proposed a measure for championship uncertainty (*UCS*). The UCS is positive if the difference between points needed to win the

Appendix   113

championship in a respective season (c_{CS}) and the number of points a team has already gained (g) is smaller than the difference between the maximum number of points a team can collect during the season (m) and the maximum number of points a team could have collected until a specific match day ($3t$):

$$UCS = f(x) = \begin{cases} \dfrac{100}{c_{CS} - g}, & \text{if } c_{CS} - g \leq m - 3t, \\ 0 \ otherwise. \end{cases} \tag{A.2}$$

With regard to match or short-term uncertainty, sports economists usually rely on betting odds as a sophisticated and unbiased predictor of match outcomes (see Peel & Thomas, 1992). Unfortunately, betting odds for the FBL are not available for the period under study. Therefore, as a rather rough proxy of match outcome uncertainty, the difference in league positions between the home and the away teams was calculated (*Difference*). Yet, *Difference* proved to be highly correlated with *HomeRank* ($r = 0.705$; $p < 0.001$) and *AwayRank* ($r = 0.706$, $p < 0.001$). Thus in order to avoid multicollinearity problems, two dummy variables were created: *David* refers to constellations where the home team competes against a much better ranked away team (*Difference* ≥ 5), *Goliath* indicates constellations where the home appears to be superior to the away team (*Difference* ≤ -5).

A further set of indicators created aims to pay attention to the home team's site characteristics. First, it was taken into account that some women's teams have changed their club affiliation in order to adapt to the organizational challenges of first-tier league soccer (see Chapter 3). Second, stadium quality was determined. Retrieving information on stadium quality proved to be cumbersome since neither the DFB nor the teams keep detailed records. Based on news reports, Internet searches, and stadium pictures, six different levels of stadium quality could be distinguished. The classification was based on the idea that spectators prefer larger, single-purpose venues with at least some spectator facilities. Accordingly, the lowest stadium quality (*Quality1*) was assigned to traditional sports grounds without any terraces or spectator facilities but with running tracks around the field. The highest quality (*Quality6*) was coded for pure football stadiums with a crowd capacity of more than 3,500 spectators. In detail, the dummy variables were defined as follows:

- *Quality1*: small sports ground without terraces or spectator facilities
- *Quality2*: small multipurpose sports ground with some terrace constructions

114   *Appendix*

- *Quality3*: smaller football stadium without seated terraces
- *Quality4*: smaller football stadium with seated terraces
- *Quality5*: multipurpose stadium with a crowd capacity of more than 3500
- *Quality6*: football stadium with a crowd capacity of more than 3500

The urbanity of the home team site was operationalized by regional population density in the county of the home team (*Density*). A correlation between *Density* and *Season* seemed to suggest that there exists a slight long-term trend toward more urban host sites ($r = 0.115$; $p < 0.001$). However, a closer inspection of the data reveals that the positive trend reflects a substantial increase in population density in Munich over the period examined.

Measuring regional income has been difficult since no consistent time series on GDP on a county level for the entire period under scrutiny exists. GDP data for German counties are only available from 2000 (see Regionalstatistik, 2014a). However, the statistical offices of the federal states provide county level data on 'Available income of private households including non-profit organizations per capita' since 1995 (Regionalstatistik, 2014b). Unfortunately, the method for calculating the indicator has been revised in 2007. However, income data calculated by both methods are available for the period between 2000 and 2007. An analysis based on all German counties for which complete data exist proved the two indicators to be highly correlated ($r = 0.944$, $p < 0.001$, n = 2,576). Therefore, minor inconsistencies were accepted and the two time series data were combined as follows: for the period before 2000, the income variable represents values calculated according to the old method, whereas for the period after 2000, the new method applies. In a second step, these nominal income data were transformed into real income (*Real income*) by adjusting for consumer price inflation (Statistisches Bundesamt, 2018). There is no substantial trend toward wealthier host sites. The weak correlation between *Real income* and *Season* ($r = 0.093$; $p < 0.001$) reflects rather a general increase in *Real income* across all host sites.

Given the lack of reliable historical data, no ticket price data indicator could be included. In order to account for traveling costs for away fans, a variable for the geographical distance between the home and away teams was created (*Distance*). Opportunity costs were operationalized with a dummy for matches staged on Saturdays and Sundays (*Weekend*). Since most matches in the FBL are played in the late morning, dummies for matches beginning in the afternoon (3 pm to 6.30 pm) (*Afternoon*) and for evening matches beginning later than 7 pm

(Evening) were included. The amount of rainfall was recoded according to common conventions (*Rain*):

- *No rain*: No rain at all
- *Slight*: 0.1 to 0.5 mm precipitation per hour
- *Moderate*: 0.5 to 4.0 mm precipitation per hour
- *Strong*: More than 4.0 mm precipitation per hour

The coding of the temperature data distinguished between four categories (*Temperature*):

- *Cold*: Below 0°C
- *Low*: Warmer than 0°C and lower than or equal to 10°C
- *Warm*: Warmer than 10°C and lower than or equal to 20°C
- *Very warm*: Warmer than 20°C

In order to account for trends in attendance, a simple variable for counting the seasons was initially created (*Season*). However, since *Season* proved to be correlated with a number of other independent variables, in particular with the habit persistence indicators, a semi-parametric approach was adopted. Accordingly, *Season* was coded as a set of distinct seasonal dummies in order to avoid multicollinearity problems. This treatment of *Season* allows for detecting non-linear trends and for tracing the impact of achievements of the national women's soccer team on FBL attendance.

In addition, two dummy variables were coded in order to account for the short-term impact of national team success on league attendance. The first variable *AfterTitle3* assumes an effect for the first three match days at the beginning of a season following a title win. Accordingly, the second variable *AfterTitle6* assumes an effect for six match days. Summary statistics for the dependent and independent variables are provided in Table A.5.

Modeling approach

The modeling approach followed the suggestion of Forrest and Simmons (2006), which was to organize the dataset as a cross-sectional time series in which home teams serve as cross-sectional units and the match number as the time variable. Since Hausman-tests suggested that individual specific effects were not unrelated, a fixed effects panel regression was used. Accordingly, the parameters estimated are consistent but might not be fully efficient. As attendance data

Table A.5 Stadium attendance in the Frauen-Bundesliga: Dependent and independent variables

Variable	Definition	N	Mean	SD	Min	Max
Attendance$_t$	Stadium attendance for the home team at t	2,507	700.473	780.791	30	12,464
Attendance$_{t-1}$	Stadium attendance for the home team at t-1	2,457	700.920	781.994	30	12,464
AwayAttendance$_{t-1}$	Stadium attendance for the away team at t-1	2,458	692.126	765.243	30	12,464
MeanHomeAtt$_{Season-1}$	Average annual stadium attendance for home team in the previous season	1,969	732.401	567.939	101.364	2,932.818
MeanAwayAtt $_{Season-1}$	Average annual stadium attendance for home team in the previous season	1,980	706.463	411.393	184.546	2,509.909
Aftertitle3	Dummy variable for the first three match days at the beginning of a season following the win of an international title by the women's national team.	2,508	0.043	0.202	0	1
Aftertitle6	Dummy variable for the first six match days at the beginning of a season following the win of an international title by the women's national team.	2,508	0.084	0.277	0	1
Stadium quality[a]						
Quality2	Small multipurpose sports ground with some terrace constructions	2,508	0.077	0.267	0	1
Quality3	Smaller football stadium without seated terraces	2,508	0.110	0.313	0	1
Quality4	Smaller football stadium with seated terraces	2,508	0.123	0.329	0	1
Quality5	Multipurpose stadium with a crowd capacity of more than 3,500	2,508	0.371	0.483	0	1

		N	Mean	SD	Min	Max
Quality6	Football stadium with a crowd capacity of more than 3500	2,508	0.275	0.447	0	1
RealIncome[b]	Real incomes of private households per capita in €1,000 in prizes of 1998	2,497	15.930	1.953	12.31	21.520
Density	Population density in home team county in inhabitants per km²	2,507	1,581.445	1,194.343	87.925	4,712.91
Independence	Dummy variable for teams that have seceded from male-dominated clubs	2,508	0.189	0.391	0	1
Switch	Dummy variable for teams that merged with established men's clubs	2,118	0.068	0.251	0	1
HomeRank	League rank of the home team	2,486	6.425	3.482	1	12
AwayRank	League rank of the away team	2,492	6.378	3.467	1	12
UCS_{Home}	Index for the probability of the home team to win the championship	2,508	2.759	5.964	0	100
UCS_{Away}	Index for the probability of the away team to win the championship	2,508	2.716	5.361	0	100
Goliath	HomeRank—AwayRank ≥ 5	2,508	0.183	0.387	0	1
David	HomeRank–AwayRank ≤ -5	2,508	0.192	0.394	0	1
Weekend	Dummy variable for matches played on Saturday and Sunday	2,508	0.895	0.307	0	1
Afternoon	Dummy variable for matches played in the afternoon	2,508	0.039	0.195	0	1
Evening	Dummy variable for matches played in the evening	2,508	0.016	0.124	0	1
Distance	Distance between home and away team in 100 km	2,508	2.979	1.432	0.007	6.440
Temperature[c]	Temperature on match day in °C					
Low		2,508	0.417	0.493	0	1
Warm		2,508	0.474	0.499	0	1
Very warm		2,508	0.059	0.236	0	1

(continued)

Table A.5 (*Cont.*)

Variable	Definition	N	Mean	SD	Min	Max
Rain[d]	Set of dummy variable for rain					
Slight	0.1 to 0.5 mm per hour	2,508	0.102	0.303	0	1
Moderate	0.5 to 4.0 mm per hour	2,508	0.171	0.376	0	1
Strong	More than 4.0 mm per hour	2,508	0.110	0.313	0	1
Season[e]	Set of dummy variables for seasons.					
1999/2000		2,508	0.053	0.223	0	1
2000/2001		2,508	0.053	0.223	0	1
2001/2002 (EURO win)		2,508	0.053	0.223	0	1
2002/2003		2,508	0.053	0.223	0	1
2003/2004 (WC win)		2,508	0.053	0.223	0	1
2004/2005		2,508	0.053	0.223	0	1
2005/2006 (EURO win)		2,508	0.053	0.223	0	1
2006/2007		2,508	0.053	0.223	0	1
2007/2008 (WC win)		2,508	0.053	0.223	0	1
2008/2009		2,508	0.053	0.223	0	1
2009/2010 (EURO win)		2,508	0.053	0.223	0	1
2010/2011		2,508	0.053	0.223	0	1
2011/2012 ('Home' WC)		2,508	0.053	0.223	0	1
2012/2013		2,508	0.053	0.223	0	1
2013/2014 (EURO win)		2,508	0.053	0.223	0	1
2014/2015		2,508	0.053	0.223	0	1
2015/2016		2,508	0.053	0.223	0	1
2016/2017 (Olympic win)		2,508	0.053	0.223	0	1

Note: a. Reference category is 'Small sports ground without terraces or spectator facilities'. b. No income statistics were available for the municipality of Leipzig in 2011. c. Reference category is 'Below 0°C'. d. Reference category is 'No rain at all'. e. Reference category is the season of 1998/1999.

Appendix 119

proved to be right-skewed, they were logarithmized (*ln Attendance$_t$*, *ln Attendance$_{t-1}$*, *ln AwayAttendance$_{t-1}$*, *MeanHomeAtt$_{Season-1}$* and *ln MeanAwayAtt$_{Season-1}$*).

As it has been assumed that women's soccer represents a niche product for diehard fans, the first models include only habit persistence indicators. Due to the fact that the inclusion of medium-term habit indicators reduced the number of cases for the analyses, two separate models were estimated, one without these medium-term habit indicators and one including them. As the medium-term habit indicators were substantially correlated with *Season*, the *Season* dummies were removed from the model. In a next step, predictors accounting for host site characteristics and quality features of sports entertainment were included. Concerning host site characteristics, one-year lags were applied for *Density* and *Real income* to account for the time needed to affect demand. Again these models were estimated both without and with the medium-term habit persistence indicators.

Chapter 4

Data sources

For the research presented in Chapter 4, a unique dataset on all live telecasts of matches of the women's national soccer team has been purchased from Media Control. Media Control markets the TV ratings gathered by the 'Gesellschaft für Konsumforschung' (GfK). GfK conducts representative TV ratings for the entire German TV industry based on an annually reviewed representative sample of 5,640 German and European Union citizen TV households, which comprises around 13,000 persons in total. GfK's estimates take into account what equipment is used to play the program. The identity and number of people watching the program is recorded by a device that can only be described as an 'active peoplemeter' (GfK Fernsehforschung, 2012). In order to scrutinize the validity of its TV ratings, GfK conducts external and internal coincidental checks (Hofsümmer, 2010; Klemm, 2010). According to internal coincidence checks, 90.7 percent of TV watchers use their personalized push button correctly (Klemm, 2010). Unfortunately, Media Control only allows access to completely anonymized aggregate data for secondary research (Meier & Leinwather, 2013).

The dataset includes ratings for all 250 matches of the women's national soccer team between January 1, 1995 and December 31, 2017. Data on match characteristics were retrieved from the official

120   *Appendix*

webpage of the DFB (www.dfb.de/frauen-nationalmannschaft/start/). The FIFA rankings of the involved teams were gathered from the official FIFA website (http://de.fifa.com/fifa-world-ranking/ranking-table/women/index.html). Weather data were conducted by relying on statistics provided by the German Meteorological Office (Deutscher Wetterdienst—DWD).

The dataset

The dependent variables analyzed here represent regional TV ratings for the matches of the women's national soccer team. These ratings have been stratified according to a number of theoretically identified criteria. In order to account for a possible influence of policy legacies in reunified Germany, the TV ratings for the matches were first stratified on the basis of the 16 federal states. In addition, TV ratings were differentiated according to biological sex. As discussed in Chapter 4, TV ratings data leave little alternative to stratifying the data according to the audiences' biological sex. Since it has been assumed that younger cohorts should be more likely to watch women's sport, the following socio-demographic groups were defined: 'Younger women': women up to 50 years, 'Older women': women 51 years and older, 'Older men': men up to 50 years, and 'Older men': men 51 years and older. Implementing a more fine-grained distinction of age groups proved to be infeasible, as the regional sample sizes would have become too small. In sum, the dataset comprises 15,998 observations on TV ratings for matches of the women's soccer team (250 matches × 16 federal states × 4 socio-demographic groups – 2 missing observations). For the multivariate analyses, the dataset was split according to the socio-demographic groups in order to account for potential differences in demand.

As in the study of stadium attendance, the approach for coding control variables follows the conventions of empirical sports economics, which have demonstrated that specific quality factors determine the demand for sports entertainment. These quality features are sporting relevance, athletic quality, and uncertainty of outcome (Borland & MacDonald, 2003; Buraimo, 2008; García & Rodríguez, 2009).

The coding of sporting relevance relies on the competitive hierarchy of women's soccer in which continental championships, such as the UEFA EURO tournaments, and ultimately the world championships, that is, the FIFA World Cup, occupy the top echelons. Moreover, in women's soccer, Olympic tournaments seem to enjoy a specific prestige. In addition to indicators for tournaments, relevance is defined by the

Appendix 121

tournament stages. As a result, a set of dummy variables was created in order to account for sporting relevance:

- *Qualification*: All qualification matches for EURO and World Cup tournaments.
- *Olympic group*: All group matches played during the Olympic soccer tournaments.
- *Olympic final.* Matches played in advanced stages of the Olympic soccer tournaments.
- *Euro group*: All group matches played during the EURO tournaments.
- *Euro final*: All matches played in advanced stages of the EURO tournaments.
- *World group*: All group matches played during the World Cup tournaments.
- *World Cup final*: All matches played in advanced stages of the World Cup tournaments.

With regard to athletic quality, FIFA rankings serve as indicators of athletic quality. However, Germany's FIFA ranking showed only a slight variance as the team always occupied either the first or the second rank. Therefore, only the FIFA rankings of the teams that Germany confronted have been considered, as elaborated below. These opponent team rankings served as the basis for a set of dummy variables on team quality. Since FIFA rankings for the women's national soccer team have only been available since July 16, 2003, separate analyses with and without the quality indicator were conducted.

Regarding match outcome uncertainty, the study follows the basic idea of using differences in team rankings as an indicator (Meier & Leinwather, 2012, 2013). The assumption is that the smaller the difference in team rankings, the more uncertain the match outcome is. Given the fact that the FIFA ranking of the German national team did not vary much over the period examined, it hardly makes sense to calculate the difference in FIFA rankings. Finally, it was decided to code a set of dummy variables on opponent ranking as an indicator for both quality and match outcome uncertainty.

- *High quality*: German opponent team occupies a FIFA rank from 1 to 5.
- *Medium*: German opponent team occupies a FIFA rank from 6 to 19.
- *Low*: German opponent team occupies a FIFA rank of 20 or higher.

122   *Appendix*

As matches of the women's national soccer team have been exclusively broadcast by public service networks, only opportunity costs are considered. Opportunity costs for free-to-air telecasts are usually measured by indicators of scheduling and weather conditions (Meier & Leinwather, 2012, 2013). Thus, dummies for *Prime Time* and *Weekend* were coded. Moreover, data on regional weather conditions for all 16 federal states were retrieved. The data used here reflect the weather conditions in the capital of the federal states at the time of kick-off. The amount of rainfall was recoded according to common conventions (*Rain*),

- *No rain*: No rain at all
- *Slight*: 0.1 to 0.5 mm precipitation per hour
- *Moderate*: 0.5 to 4.0 mm precipitation per hour
- *Strong*: More than 4.0 mm precipitation per hour

The coding of the temperature data distinguished between four categories (*Temperature*):

- *Cold*: Below 0°C
- *Low*: Warmer than 0°C and lower than or equal to 10°C
- *Warm*: Warmer than 10°C and lower than or equal to 20°C
- *Very warm*: Warmer than 20°C

As measures of the public visibility of the team, dummies for home matches (*Home*) and telecasts on major networks (*Major Networks*) were included.

The years in which the matches were broadcast served as the basis for the creation of a trend indicator. However, given the fact that the 'home' World Cup of 2011 created unusual media attention and might have had a rather ambiguous effect on the popularity of women's soccer, a semi-parametric modeling approach seemed more appropriate. Accordingly, years have been coded as a set of dummy variables.

Furthermore, in order to examine the potential socialization effects of the different gender regimes in West and East Germany, a simple dummy variable for East Germany was created (*East*). In order to adress the questions of whether there is convergence or divergence between TV consumption patterns in West and East Germany, interaction effects between these year dummy variables and *East* were modeled. Table A.6 provides definitions and descriptive statistics for all dependent and independent variables.

Table A.6 Popularity of the women's national soccer team: Dependent and independent variables

Variable	Definition	N	Mean	SD	Min	Max
Younger women	TV share among women between 3 and 50 years	4,000	6.7443	9.193	0.000	63.442
Younger men	TV share among men between 3 and 50 years	4,000	12.354	12.875	0.000	80.150
Older women	TV share among women older than 50 years	4,000	13.801	11.592	0.000	82.703
Older men	TV share among men older than 50 years	3,998	28.974	17.451	0.000	87.704
Athletic relevance[a]	Set of dummy variables for the athletic relevance of matches					
Qualification	Qualification matches	4,000	0.276	0.447	0	1
Olympic Group	Olympic tournament group matches	4,000	0.052	0.222	0	1
Olympic Final	Olympic tournament final matches	4,000	0.044	0.205	0	1
EURO Group	EURO tournament group matches	4,000	0.068	0.252	0	1
EURO Final	EURO tournament final matches	4,000	0.052	0.222	0	1
World Cup Group	World Cup group matches	4,000	0.064	0.245	0	1
World Cup Final	World Cup final matches	4,000	0.060	0.238	0	1
Opponent quality[b]	Set of dummy variables for FIFA ranking of the opponent team					
Medium	Rank 6 to 19	3,008	0.410	0.492	0	1
Low	Rank 20 and higher	3,008	0.335	0.472	0	1
East[c]	Dummy variable for East German federal states	4,000	0.313	0.464	0	1
Year[d]	Set of dummy variables for years					
1996		4,000	0.016	0.125	0	1
1997		4,000	0.024	0.153	0	1
1998		4,000	0.008	0.089	0	1
1999		4,000	0.032	0.176	0	1
2000		4,000	0.036	0.186	0	1
2001		4,000	0.036	0.186	0	1

(continued)

Table A.6 (Cont.)

Variable	Definition	N	Mean	SD	Min	Max
2002		4,000	0.016	0.125	0	1
2003		4,000	0.072	0.259	0	1
2004		4,000	0.060	0.238	0	1
2005		4,000	0.040	0.196	0	1
2006		4,000	0.052	0.222	0	1
2007		4,000	0.068	0.252	0	1
2008		4,000	0.060	0.238	0	1
2009		4,000	0.064	0.245	0	1
2010		4,000	0.020	0.140	0	1
2011		4,000	0.052	0.222	0	1
2012		4,000	0.040	0.196	0	1
2013		4,000	0.092	0.289	0	1
2014		4,000	0.036	0.186	0	1
2015		4,000	0.072	0.259	0	1
2016		4,000	0.056	0.230	0	1
2017		4,000	0.032	0.176	0	1
Home[e]	Dummy variable for home matches	4,000	0.436	0.496	0	1
Major[f]	Dummy variable for matches shown on a major network	4,000	0.856	0.351	0	1
Weekend[g]	Dummy variable for matches shown on weekends	4,000	0.276	0.447	0	1
Prime Time[h]	Dummy variable for prime-time matches (07.30 p.m.—11.00 p.m.)	4,000	0.092	0.289	0	1
Season[i]	Set of dummy for seasons				0	1
Summer		4,000	0.376	0.484	0	1
Fall		4,000	0.320	0.467	0	1
Winter		4,000	0.040	0.196	0	1

Temperature[j]	Set of dummy variables for temperature					
Low	Temperature 0 to 10°C	4,000	0.243	0.429	0	1
Warm	Temperature 10 to 20°C	4,000	0.512	0.500	0	1
Very warm	Temperature higher than 20°C	4,000	0.211	0.408	0	1
Rain[k]	Set of dummy variable for rain					
Slight	0.1 to 0.5 mm per hour	4,000	0.062	0.242	0	1
Moderate	0.5 to 4.0 mm per hour	4,000	0.042	0.201	0	1
Strong	More than 4.0 mm per hour	4,000	0.008	0.086	0	1

Notes: a. Reference category is 'Friendlies'. b. Reference category is 'Top', that is, opponent teams occupying FIFA ranks 1 to 5. c. Reference category is West Germany. d. Reference category is '1995'. e. Reference category is 'Away match'. f. Reference category is special interest or regional network. g. Reference category is workdays (Monday to Friday). h. Reference category is all other time slots. i. Reference category is 'Spring'. j. Reference category is 'Below 0°C'. k. Reference category is 'No rain at all'.

Appendix

Modeling approach

The differences between the distinct socio-demographic groups could be straightforwardly examined by using mean comparisons and analysis of variance (ANOVA). However, tracing trends over time required more complex multivariate analyses. Accordingly, separate analyses for the distinct socio-demographic groups were conducted. Since the dataset consists of repeated observations (TV ratings) on individual units (federal states) over time (matches), the analyses deal with panel data. The time-series-cross-section character of the data implies potentially complex error structures. Data analysis is further complicated by the fact that the dependent variable is heavily right-skewed (Figure A.1).

Square root transformation emerged as the appropriate procedure for mitigating this right-skewedness. However, rather than using a nonlinear transformation of the dependent variable, a generalized estimating equation (GEE) approach was employed. A GEE approach is particularly suitable for analyzing longitudinal, nested, or repeated measures. GEEs use the generalized linear model to estimate more efficient and unbiased regression parameters than ordinary least squares

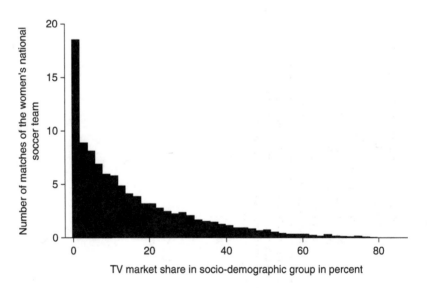

Figure A.1 Histogram of TV ratings for matches of the women's national soccer team

Note: N = 15,998.

Source: Media Control/GfK.

regression. However, fitting a GEE model requires the following to be specified: (a) a link function to be used; (b) the distribution of the dependent variable; and (c) the correlation structure of the dependent variable (Ballinger, 2004), as explained below:

(a) For the link function, a linear combination of the covariates was assumed.
(b) In the distribution of the dependent variable, a square-root transformation was specified.
(c) In order to identify a working correlation matrix, the approach employed here followed Hardin and Hilbe (2013), who suggested using the quasi-likelihood under the independence model information criterion (QIC) as proposed by Pan (2001).

According to the estimates, the correlation structure for the within-group correlation was independent. Furthermore, the QIC_u was used to select the best model (Hardin & Hilbe, 2013: 210). The estimates suggested that the QIC_u was lowest when all explanatory variables were included in the models (Tables A.7 to A.14).

Table A.7 Determining correlation structure—women between 3 and 50 years

Correlation	Variables	QIC
Exchangeable	All	219,382.550
Independent	All	**1,791,73.209**
Unstructured	All	---
Autoregressive	All	179,325.311
Stationary	All	198,013.725
Non-stationary	All	---

Note: --- = no convergence achieved.

Table A.8 Determining model—women between 3 and 50 years

Model	QIC_u
Athletic quality only	262,138.560
Athletic quality, East and Trends	238,951.965
Athletic quality, East, Trends and visibility	209,325.478
Athletic quality, East, Trends, visibility and opportunity costs	**179,151.067**

Table A.9 Determining correlation structure—women older than 50 years

Correlation	Variables	QIC
Exchangeable	All	306,260.562
Independent	All	**293,070.995**
Unstructured	All	---
Autoregressive	All	294,991.387
Stationary	All	294,540.807
Non-stationary	All	---

Note: --- = no convergence achieved.

Table A.10 Determining model—women older than 50 years

Model	QIC_u
Athletic quality only	438,070.737
Athletic quality, East and Trends	396,200.587
Athletic quality, East, Trends and visibility	307,993.239
Athletic quality, East, Trends, visibility and opportunity costs	**293,000.384**

Table A.11 Determining correlation structure—men between 3 and 50 years

Correlation	Variables	QIC
Exchangeable	All	373,795.967
Independent	All	**367,148.138**
Unstructured	All	---
Autoregressive	All	367,700.128
Stationary	All	367,569.786
Non-stationary	All	---

Note: --- = no convergence achieved.

Table A.12 Determining model—men between 3 and 50 years

Model	QIC_u
Athletic quality only	507,017.553
Athletic quality, East and Trends	478,590.460
Athletic quality, East, Trends and visibility	415,161.205
Athletic quality, East, Trends, visibility and opportunity costs	**367,118.633**

Table A.13 Determining correlation structure—men older than 50 years

Correlation	Variables	QIC
Exchangeable	All	637,822.639
Independent	All	**614,739.546**
Unstructured	All	---
Autoregressive	All	619,856.465
Stationary	All	619,487.827
Non-stationary	All	---

Note: --- = no convergence achieved.

Table A.14 Determining model—men older than 50 years

Model	QIC_u
Athletic quality only	973,204.501
Athletic quality, East and Trends	908,351.740
Athletic quality, East, Trends and visibility	626,459.599
Athletic quality, East, Trends, visibility and opportunity costs	**614,661.780**

References

Adler, M. A. & Brayfield, A. (1997). Women's work values in unified Germany: Regional differences as remnants of the past. *Work and Occupations, 24*, 245–266.

Akerlof, G. A., Rose, A. K., Yellen, J. L., Hessenius, H., Dornbusch, R., & Guitian, M. (1991). East Germany in from the cold: The economic aftermath of currency union. *Brookings Papers on Economic Activity, 1991*(1), 1–105.

Andreß, H. J. & Heien, T. (2001). Four worlds of welfare state attitudes? A comparison of Germany, Norway, and the United States. *European Sociological Review, 17*(4), 337–356.

Atherley, K. M. (2006). Sport, localism and social capital in rural Western Australia. *Geographical Research, 44*(4), 348–360.

Baimbridge, M., Cameron, S., & Dawson, P. (1996). Satellite television and the demand for football: A whole new ball game? *Scottish Journal of Political Economy, 43*(3), 317–333.

Balbier, U. A. (2007). *Kalter Krieg auf der Aschenbahn: Der deutsch-deutsche Sport 1950–1972: Eine politische Geschichte*. Paderborn: Schöning.

Bale, J. (2003). *Sports Geography*. London: Routledge.

Ballinger, G. A. (2004). Using generalized estimating equations for longitudinal data analysis. *Organizational Research Methods, 7*(2), 127–150.

Barroso, A., Giarratana, M. S., Reis, S., & Sorenson, O. (2016). Crowding, satiation, and saturation: The days of television series' lives. *Strategic Management Journal, 37*(3), 565–585.

Barth, A. & Trübner, M. (2018). Structural stability, quantitative change: A latent class analysis approach towards gender role attitudes in Germany. *Social Science Research, 72*(1), 183–193.

Bauernschuster, S. & Rainer, H. (2011). Political regimes and the family: How sex-roles continue to differ in unified Germany. *Journal of Population Economy, 25*(1), 5–27.

Baum, J. A. C. & Amburgey, T. L. (2002). Organizational ecology. In J.A.C. Baum (eds), *The Blackwell Companion to Organizations* (pp. 304–326). Oxford, UK: Blackwell.

Becker, C. & Buss, W. (2006). Das 'Wunder von Bern' und die DDR. *Deutschland Archiv, 37*(3), 389–399.

References 131

Becker, F. (1994). Die Sportlerin als Vorbild der 'neuen Frau': Versuche zur Umwertung der Geschlechterrollen in der Weimarer Republik. *Sozial- und Zeitgeschichte des Sports, 8*(1), 34–55.

Benz, M.-A., Brandes, L., & Franck, E. (2009). Do soccer associations really spend on a good thing? Empirical evidence on heterogeneity in the consumer response to match uncertainty of outcome. *Contempory Economic Policy, 27*(2), 216–235.

Berkowitz, J. P., Depken, C. A., & Wilson, D. P. (2011). When going in circles is going backward: Outcome uncertainty in NASCAR. *Journal of Sport Economics, 12*(3), 253–283.

Bernard, A. B. & Busse, M. R. (2004). Who wins the Olympic Games: Economic resources and medal totals. *Review of Economics and Statistics, 86*(1), 413–417.

Berri, D. J., Schmidt, M. B., & Brook, S. L. (2004). Stars at the gate: The impact of star power on NBA gate revenues. *Journal of Sports Economics, 5*(1), 33–50.

Bird, P. J. W. N. (1982). The demand for league football. *Applied Economics, 14*(6), 637–649.

BMI (Bundeministerium des Innern) (2014a). *Demografiebericht: Bericht der Bundesregierung zur demografischen Lage und künftigen Entwicklung des Landes.* Berlin: BMI.

BMI (Bundeministerium des Innern) (2014b). *Demography Report: Federal Government Report on the Demographic Situation and Future Development of Germany.* Berlin: BMI.

BMWi (Bundesministerium für Wirtschaft und Energie) (2017). *Jahresbericht der Bundesregierung zum Stand der Deutschen Einheit 2017.* Berlin: BMWi.

Borland, J. & Lye, J. (1992). Attendance at Australian Rules football: A panel study. *Applied Economics, 24*(9), 1053–1058.

Borland, J. & MacDonald, R. (2003). Demand for sport. *Oxford Review of Economic Policy, 19*(4), 478–502.

Boyle, R. (2014). Television sport in the age of screens and content. *Television & New Media, 15*(8), 746–751.

Brandes, L. & Franck, E. (2007). Who made who? An empirical analysis of competitive balance in European soccer leagues. *Eastern Economic Journal, 33*(3), 379–403.

Brandes, L., Franck, E., & Nüesch, S. (2008). Local heroes and superstars. An empirical analysis of star attraction in German soccer. *Journal of Sport Economics, 9*(3), 266–286.

Brändle, F. & Koller, C. (2002). *Goal. Kultur-und Sozialgeschichte des modernen Fußballs.* Zürich: Orell Füssli.

Braun, M., Scott, J. & Alwyn, D. F. (1994). Economic necessity or self-actualization? Attitudes toward women's labour-force participation in East and West Germany. *European Sociological Review, 10*(1), 29–47.

Breuer, C. & Feiler, S. (2017). *Sportentwicklungsbericht 2015/2016. Analyse zur Situation der Sportvereine in Deutschland.* Köln: Sportverlag Strauß.

132 References

Breuer, M. (2009). The demand for football tickets depending on the number of clubs in a city: Empirical evidence from Germany. Working Paper No. 2009.5. International Network for Economic Research. Available at: https://ideas.repec.org/p/inf/wpaper/2009.5.html.

Bruggeman, J., Grunow, D., Leenders, M., Vermeulen, I., & Kuilman, J. G. (2012). Market positioning: The shifting effects of niche overlap. *Industrial and Corporate Change, 21*(6), 1451–1477.

Brüggemeier, F. J. (2004). *Zurück auf dem Platz: Deutschland und die Fußball-Weltmeisterschaft 1954.* München: Deutsche Verlags-Anstalt.

Brüggemeier, F. J. (2006). Das "Fußballwunder" von 1954. *Informationen zur politischen Bildung, 290*, 27–33.

Büch, M.-P. (1979). Modell und Realität der Fußball-Bundesliga—eine ökonomische Betrachtung. *Zeitschrift für Wirtschafts- und Sozialwissenschaften, 99*(4), 447–466.

Buchanan, T. & Buchanan, J. (1987). Rural change and social institutions: Implications for providers of leisure services. *Journal of Physical Education and Recreation, 28*(4), 3–4.

Budde, G.-F. (2000). Der Körper der "sozialistischen Frauenpersönlichkeit": Weiblichkeitvorstellungen in der SBZ und frühen DDR. *Geschichte und Gesellschaft, 26*(4), 602–628.

Budig, M. J., Misra, J., & Boeckmann, I. (2016). Work–family policy trade-offs for mothers? Unpacking the cross-national variation in motherhood earnings penalties. *Work and Occupations, 43*(2), 119–177.

Buraimo, B. (2006). The demand for sports broadcasting. In A. Wladimir & S. Szymanski (eds), *Handbook on the Economics of Sport* (pp. 100–111). Cheltenham: Edward Elgar.

Buraimo, B. (2008). Stadium attendance and television audience demand in English league football. *Managerial and Decision Economics, 29*(6), 513–523.

Buraimo, B. & Simmons, R. (2008). Do sports fans really value uncertainty of outcome? Evidence from the English Premier League. *International Journal of Sport Finance, 3*(3), 146–155.

Buraimo, B. & Simmons, R. (2009). A tale of two audiences: Spectators, television viewers and outcome uncertainty in Spanish football. *Journal of Economics and Business, 61*(4), 326–338.

Burda, M. C. & Hunt, J. (2001). From reunification to economic integration: productivity and the labor market in Eastern Germany. *Brookings Papers on Economic Activity, 2001*(2), 1–92.

Busse, A. & Gathmann, C. (2018). Free daycare and its effects on children and their families. IZA Discussion Paper No. 11269.

Buytendijk, F. J. J. (1953). *Das Fußballspiel: Eine psychologische Studie.* Würzburg: Werkbund Verlag.

Cairns, J. A. (1990). The demand for professional team sports. *British Review of Economic Issues, 12*(1), 1–20.

Cairns, J. A., Jennett, N., & Sloane, P. J. (1986). The economics of professional team sports: A survey of theory and evidence. *Journal of Economic Studies, 13*(1), 3–80.

References 133

Campbell, R. (2012). Values, trust and democracy in Germany: Still in search of 'inner unity'? *European Journal of Political Research, 51*(5), 646–670.

Campbell, R. (2015). Winners, losers and the Grand Coalition: Political satisfaction in the Federal Republic of Germany. *International Political Science Review, 36*(2), 168–184.

Carmichael, F., Millington, J., & Simmons, R. (1999). Elasticity of demand for rugby league attendance and the impact of BSkyB. *Applied Economics Letters, 68*(12), 797–800.

Carroll, G. R. & Hannan, M. T. (2004). *The Demography of Corporations and Industries*. Princeton, NJ: Princeton University Press.

Caudwell, J. (2006). Femme-fatale: Rethinking the femme-nine. In J. Caudwell, *Sport, Sexualities and Queer/Theory* (pp. 145–158). New York: United States.

Cho, S. Y. (2013). A league of their own: Female soccer, male legacy and women's empowerment. Discussion Papers of DIW Berlin 1267, Berlin: Germany, German Institute for Economic Research.

Christensen, B., Christensen, S., Hoppe, T., & Spandel, M. (2015). Everything counts! *AStA Wirtschafts-und Sozialstatistisches Archiv, 9*(3–4), 215–232.

Ciccia, R. & Bleijenberg, I. (2014). After the male breadwinner model? Childcare services and the division of labor in European countries. *Social Politics: International Studies in Gender, State & Society, 21*(1), 50–79.

Coates, D., Humphreys, B. R., & Zhou, L. (2014). Reference-dependent preferences, loss aversion, and live game attendance. *Economic Inquiry, 52*(3), 959–973.

Congdon-Hohman, J. & Matheson, V. A. (2013). International women's soccer and gender inequality: Revisited. In E. M. Leeds & M. A. Leeds (eds), *Handbook on the Economics of Women in Sports* (pp. 345–364). Cheltenham: Edgar Elgar.

Cranmer, G. A., Brann, M., & Bowman, N. D. (2014). Male athletes, female aesthetics: The continued ambivalence toward female athletes in ESPN's The Body Issue. *International Journal of Sport Communication, 7*(2), 145–165.

Cunningham, G. B., Fink, J. S., & Kenix, L. J. (2008). Choosing an endorser for a women's sporting event: The interaction of attractiveness and expertise. *Sex Roles, 58*(5–6), 371.

Czarnitzki, D. & Stadtmann, G. (2002). Uncertainty of outcome versus reputation: Empirical evidence for the First German Football Division. *Empirical Economics, 27*(1), 101–112.

Da Costa, L. M. (2014). Beauty, effort and talent: A brief history of Brazilian women's soccer in press discourse. *Soccer & Society, 15*(1), 81–92.

Dalton, R. J. & Weldon, S. (2010). Germans divided? Political culture in a united Germany. *German Politics, 19*(1), 9–23.

Degele, N. (2012). The future is female—or feminine? Available at: www.gwi-boell.de/web/democracy-football-future-female-feiminine-4195.htm.

Dennis, M. & Grix, J. (2012). *Sport Under Communism: Behind the East German 'Miracle'*. New York: Palgrave Macmillan.

DFB. (2013). *Zukunftsstrategie Amateurfußball—Masterplan 2013-2016: Ziele—Handlungsfelder—Umsetzung*. Frankfurt am Main: DFB. Available at: www.flb.de/db.php/download/1004/Masterplan+Fußball-Landesverband+Brandenburg1.pdf.

134   References

Dieckhoff, M., Gash, V., Mertens, A., & Gordo, L. R. (2016). A stalled revolution? What can we learn from women's drop-out to part-time jobs: A comparative analysis of Germany and the UK. *Research in Social Stratification and Mobility, 46*(B), 129–140.

Dietz-Uhler, B., Harrick, E. A., End, C., & Jacquemotte, L. (2000). Sex differences in sport fan behavior and reasons for being a sport fan. *Journal of Sport Behavior, 23*(3), 219.

Dobson, S. M. & Goddard, J. A. (1996). The demand for football in the regions of England and Wales. *Regional Studies, 30*(5), 443–453.

DOSB (2016). *Bestandserhebung 2016: Aktualisierte Fassung vom 1. November 2016: Stichtag der Erfassung: 1. Januar 2016*. Frankfurt am Main: DOSB.

DOSB (2018). *Bestandserhebung 2017: Aktualisierte Fassung vom 25. Januar 2018: Stichtag der Erfassung: 1. Januar 2017*. Frankfurt am Main: DOSB.

Downward, P. & Dawson, A. (2000). *The Economics of Professional Team Sport.* London: Routledge.

Dunn, C. (2016). *Football and the Women's World Cup: Organisation, Media and Fandom.* Houndmills: Palgrave.

Eder, M. (2018). 'Vereine können ein Anker sein': Der Winzer, Gastronom und Hotelier Fritz Keller sieht als Präsident des SC Freiburg die Klubs in einer 'Wahnsinnsverantwortung'. Mit einem ganzheitlichen Erziehungsauftrag lehre der Sport den Diskurs in einer polarisierten Welt. *Frankfurter Allgemeine Zeitung*, November 4, p. 44.

Edlund, L. (2005). Sex and the city. *Scandinavian Journal of Economics, 107*(1), 25–44.

Eisenberg, C. (1997). Deutschland. In C. Eisenberg (ed.), *Fußball, Soccer, Calcio: Ein Englischer Sport auf seinem Weg um die Welt* (pp. 94–129). München: DTV.

European Commission (2017). *Women in the Labour Market: European Semester Thematic Factsheet*. Brussels: European Commission.

Eurostat (2018). Gender pay gap statistics. *Eurostat*. Available at: https://ec.europa.eu/eurostat/statistics-explained/pdfscache/6776.pdf.

Feddersen, A. & Maennig, W. (2007). Arenas vs. multifunctional stadia—Which do spectators prefer? *Hamburg Contemporary Economic Discussion, 14*.

Feddersen, A. & Rott, A. (2011). Determinants of demand for televised live football: Features of the German national football team. *Journal of Sports Economics, 12*(3), 352–369.

Feddersen, A., Maennig, W., & Borcherding, M. (2006). The novelty effect of new soccer stadia: The case of Germany. *International Journal of Sport Finance, 1*(3), 174–188.

Feehan, P. (2006). Attendance at sports events. In W. Andreff & S. Szymanski (eds), *Handbook on the Economics of Sport* (pp. 90–99). Cheltenham: Edward Elgar.

Ferreira, M. & Bravo, G. (2007). A multilevel model analysis of professional soccer attendance in Chile 1990–2002. *International Journal of Sports Marketing and Sponsorship, 8*(3), 49–66.

References 135

FIFA (2011). Message from the FIFA President on International Women's Day. Available at: www.fifa.com/about-fifa/who-we-are/news/message-from-the-fifa-president-international-women-day-1393938.

Fink, J. S. (2008). Gender and sex diversity in sport organizations: Concluding comments. *Sex Roles, 58*(1–2), 146–147.

Fink, J. S. (2015). Female athletes, women's sport, and the sport media commercial complex: Have we really 'come a long way, baby'? *Sport Management Review, 18*(3), 331–342.

Fink, J. S., Cunningham, G. B., & Kensicki, L. J. (2004). Using athletes as endorsers to sell women's sport: Attractiveness vs. expertise. *Journal of Sport Management, 18*(4), 350–367.

Fink, J. S., Trail, G. T., & Anderson, D. F. (2002). Environmental factors associated with spectator attendance and sport consumption behavior: Gender and team differences. *Sport Marketing Quarterly, 11*, 8–19.

Forrest, D. & Simmons, R. (2002). Outcome uncertainty and attendance demand in sport: The case of English soccer. *Statistician, 51*(2), 229–241.

Forrest, D. & Simmons, R. (2006). New issues in attendance demand: The case of the English Football League. *Journal of Sports Economics, 7*(3), 247–266.

Forrest, D., Simmons, R., & Buraimo, B. (2005). Outcome uncertainty and the couch potato audience. *Scottish Journal of Political Economy, 52*(4), 641–661.

Fort, R. D. (2004). Inelastic sports pricing. *Managerial and Decision Economics, 25*(2), 87–94.

Frankfurter Allgemeine Zeitung (2005). Schröder möchte mehr Frauen-Fußball sehen. *Frankfurter Allgemeine Zeitung*, August 31, p. 30.

Frankfurter Allgemeine Zeitung (2011). Ecke von links. Wahre Heldinnen. *Frankfurter Allgmeine Zeitung*, July 18, p. 18.

Frick, B. & Wicker, P. (2016). The trickle-down effect: How elite sporting success affects amateur participation in German football. *Applied Economics Letters, 23*(4), 259–263.

Frick, B., Lehmann, E., & Weigand, J. (1999). Kooperationserfordernisse und Wettbewerbsintensität im Team-Sport. In J. Engelhard & E. J. Sinz (eds), *Kooperation im Wettbewerb: Neue Formen und Gestaltungskonzepte im Zeichen von Globalisierung und Informationstechnologie* (pp. 497–523). Wiesbaden: Gabler.

Fuchs, M., Rossen, A., Weyh, A. & Wydra-Somaggio, G. (2019). Why do women earn more than men in some regions? Explaining regional differences in the gender pay gap in Germany. IAB-Discussion Paper, 11/2019.

Gabriel, O. W. (2007). Bürger und Demokratie im vereinigten Deutschland. *Politische Vierteljahresschrift, 48*(3), 540–552.

Gangl, M. & Ziefle, A. (2015). The making of a good woman: Extended parental leave entitlements and mothers' work commitment in Germany. *American Journal of Sociology, 121*(2), 511–563.

Gantz, W. (1981). An exploration of viewing motives and behaviors associated with television sports. *Journal of Broadcasting & Electronic Media, 25*(3), 263–275.

136 References

Gantz, W. & Wenner, L. A. (1991). Men, women, and sports: Audience experiences and effects. *Journal of Broadcasting & Electronic Media, 35*(2), 233–243.

Gantz, W. & Wenner, L. A. (1995). Fanship and the television sports viewing experience. *Sociology of Sport Journal, 12*(1), 56–74.

Gantz, W., Wang, Z., Paul, B., & Potter, R. F. (2006). Sports versus all comers: Comparing TV sports fans with fans of other programming genres. *Journal of Broadcasting & Electronic Media, 50*(1), 95–118.

García, J. & Rodríguez, P. (2002). The determinants of football match attendance revisited: Empirical evidence from the Spanish Football League. *Journal of Sports Economics, 3*(1), 18–38.

García, J. & Rodríguez, P. (2009). Sports attendance: A survey of the literature 1973–2007. *Rivista di Diritto ed Economia dello Sport, 5*(2), 111–151.

Gärtner, M. & Pommerehne, W. (1978). Der Fußball Zuschauer—Ein homo oeconomicus? Eine theoretische und empirische analyse. *Jahrbuch der Sozialwissenschaften, 29*(102), 88–107.

Geisler, E. & Kreyenfeld, M. (2005). Müttererwerbstätigkeit in Ost- und Westdeutschland: Eine Analyse mit den Mikrozensen 1991–2002. MPIDF Working Paper WP 2005–033.

Gerhard, H. & Geese, S. (2016). Die Fussball-Europameisterschaft 2016 im Fernsehen. *Media Perspektiven, 2016*(10), 491–500.

Gerhard, H. & Zubayr, C. (2014). Die Fußball-Weltmeisterschaft 2014 im Fernsehen. Daten zur Rezeption und Bewertung. *Media Perspektiven, 2014*(9), 447–455.

Haase, M., Becker, I., Nill, A., Shultz, C. J., & Gentry, J. W. (2016). Male breadwinner ideology and the inclination to establish market relationships: Model development using data from Germany and a mixed-methods research strategy. *Journal of Macromarketing, 36*(2), 149–167.

Hall, M. A. (2004). The game of choice: Girls' and women's soccer in Canada. In *Soccer, Women, Sexual Liberation* (pp. 42–59). London: Routledge.

Hallmann, K., Wicker, P., Breuer, C., & Schönherr, L. (2012). Understanding the importance of sport infrastructure for participation in different sports: Findings from multi-level modeling. *European Sport Management Quarterly, 12*(5), 525–544.

Hanel, B. & Riphan, R. T. (2011). The employment of mothers: Recent developments and their determinants in East and West Germany. IZA Discussion Paper No. 5752.

Hannan, M. T. & Freeman, J. (1977). The population ecology of organizations. *American Journal of Sociology, 82*(5), 929–964.

Hannan, M. T. & Freeman, J. (1984). Structural inertia and organizational change. *American Sociological Review, 49*(2), 149–164.

Hannan, M. T. & Freeman, J. (1989). *Organizational Ecology*. Cambridge, MA: Harvard University Press.

Hannan, M. T., Carroll, G. R. & Pólos, L. (2003). The organizational niche. *Sociological Theory, 21*(4), 309–340.

References 137

Hardin, J. W. & Hilbe, J. M. (2013). *Generalized Estimating Equations*, 2nd edn. London: Chapman and Hall.

Harris, J. (2005). The image problem in women's football. *Journal of Sport and Social Issues, 29*(2), 184–197.

Hausman, J. A. & Leonard, G. K. (1997). Superstars in the National Basketball Association: Economic value and policy. *Journal of Labor Economics, 15*(4), 586–624.

Havemann, N. (2005). *Fußball unterm Hakenkreuz: Der DFB zwischen Sport, Politik und Kommerz.* Frankfurt am Main & New York: Campus Verlag.

Heiland, F. W. (2004). Trends in East-West German migration from 1989 to 2002. *Demographic Research, 11*(7), 173–194.

Hennies, R. & Meuren, D. (2011). *Frauenfussball: Aus dem Abseits an die Spitze.* Göttingen: Verlag Die Werkstatt.

Herzog, M. (2018). The beginnings of women's football in south-western Germany: From a spectacle to a sport event. In G. Pfister & S. Pope (eds), *Female Football Players and Fans* (pp. 55–75). London: Palgrave Macmillan.

Hilbe, J. M. (2014). *Modeling Count Data.* Cambridge, UK: Cambridge University Press.

Hoekman, R., Breedveld, K., & Kraaykamp, G. (2016a). A landscape of sport facilities in the Netherlands. *International Journal of Sport Policy and Politics, 8*(2), 305–320.

Hoekman, R., Breedveld, K., & Kraaykamp, G. (2016b). Sport participation and the social and physical environment: Explaining differences between urban and rural areas in the Netherlands. *Leisure Studies, 36*(3), 1–14.

Hoffmann, E. & Nendza, J. (2006). *Verlacht, verboten und gefeiert: Zur Geschichte des Frauenfußballs in Deutschland,* 2nd edn. Weilerswist: Verlag Landpresse.

Hoffmann, R., Chew Ging, L., Matheson, V., & Ramasamy, B. (2006). International women's football and gender inequality. *Applied Economics Letters, 13*(15), 999–1001.

Hofsümmer, K.-H. (2010). Reichweitenmessung im Fernsehpanel 2010: Valide Daten für Werbung und Programm. *Media Perspektiven, 2010*(12), 588–598.

Hoggart, K. & Paniagua, A. (2001). What rural restructuring? *Journal of Rural Studies, 17*(1), 41–62.

Holsten, N. & Wörner, S. (2011). Frauenfußball-zurück aus dem Abseits. *Aus Politik und Zeitgeschichte, 16*(19), 21–26.

Hong, E. (2012). Women's football in the two Koreas: A comparative sociological analysis. *Journal of Sport and Social Issues, 36*(2), 115–134.

Horch, H. D. (1983). *Strukturbesonderheiten freiwilliger Vereinigungen: Analyse und Untersuchung einer alternativen Form menschlichen Zusammenarbeitens.* Frankfurt am Main: Campus.

Hübner, H. (2008). Einfluss der demographischen Veränderungen auf das Sportverhalten, der bestimmenden Größe für die Sportnachfrage vor Ort. In Innenministerium Nordrhein-Westfalen (ed.), *Sportstätten und Demographischer Wandel* (pp. 25–46). Düsseldorf: Innenministerium Nordrhein-Westfalen.

138   References

Huffman, M. L., King, J., & Reichelt, M. (2017). Equality for whom? Organizational policies and the gender gap across the German earnings distribution. *ILR Review*, 70(1), 16–41.

Hunt, J. (2006). Staunching emigration from East Germany: Age and the determinants of migration. *Journal of the European Economic Association*, 4(5), 1014–1037.

Hutchins, B. & Rowe, D. (2012). *Sport beyond Television: The Internet, Digital Media and the Rise of Networked Media Sport*. London: Routledge.

Ilieş, A., Dehoorne, O., Wendt, J., & Kozma, G. (2014). For geography and sport, sport geography or geography of sport. *Geosport for Society*, 1(1–2), 7–18.

Jacobs, A. M. & Weaver, R. K. (2015). When policies undo themselves: Self-undermining feedback as a source of policy change. *Governance*, 28(4), 441–457.

Jacobs, B. (2004). *The Dick, Kerr's Ladies*. London: Robinson.

Jacobs, J. C. (2014). Programme-level determinants of women's international football performance. *European Sport Management Quarterly*, 14(5), 521–537.

James, J. D. & Ridinger, L. L. (2002). Female and male sport fans: A comparison of sport consumption motives. *Journal of Sport Behavior*, 25(3), 260–278.

Janssens, P. & Késenne, S. (1987). Belgian football attendances. *Tijdschrift voor Enonomie en Management*, 32(3), 305–315.

Jinxia, D. & Mangan, J. A. (2002). Ascending then descending? Women's soccer in modern China. *Soccer & Society*, 3(2), 1–18.

Jones, J. C. H. & Ferguson, D. G. (1988). Location and survival in the National Hockey League. *Journal of Industrial Economics*, 36(4), 443–457.

Kanazawa, M. T. & Funk, J. P. (2001). Racial discrimination in professional basketball: Evidence from Nielsen ratings. *Economic Inquiry*, 39(4), 599–608.

Kane, M. J. & Maxwell, H. D. (2011). Expanding the boundaries of sport media research: Using critical theory to explore consumer responses to representations of women's sports. *Journal of Sport Management*, 25(3), 202–216.

Kane, M. J., LaVoi, N. M., & Fink, J. S. (2013). Exploring elite female athletes' interpretations of sport media images: A window into the construction of social identity and 'selling sex' in women's sports. *Communication & Sport*, 1(3), 269–298.

Kim, K. & Sagas, M. (2014). Athletic or sexy? A comparison of female athletes and fashion models in Sports Illustrated swimsuit issues. *Gender Issues*, 31(2), 123–141.

Kjær, J. B. & Agergaard, S. (2013). Understanding women's professional soccer: The case of Denmark and Sweden. *Soccer & Society*, 14(6), 816–833.

Klein, M. L. (2018). Women's football leagues in Europe: Organizational and economic perspectives. In G. Pfister & S. Pope (eds), *Female Football Players and Fans* (pp. 77–101). London: Palgrave Macmillan.

Klein, M. L., Deitersen-Wieber, A., & Lelek, S. (2012). Strukturelle Auswirkungen der Inklusion des Frauen-und Mädchenfußballs in die Fußballvereine–untersucht am Beispiel des Westdeutschen Fußball-und

References 139

Leichtathletikverbandes. In G. Sobiech & A. Ochsner (eds), *Spielen Frauen ein anderes Spiel* (pp. 61–75). Wiesbaden: VS Verlag für Sozialwissenschaften.

Klein, M. W. (2004). Work and play: International evidence of gender equality in employment and sports. *Journal of Sports Economics, 5*(3), 227–242.

Klemm, E. (2010). Qualitätsprüfung im Fernsehpanel 2010. Ergebnisse eines Internen Coincidental Checks des AGF/GfK-Fernsehpanels. *Media Perspektiven, 2010*(12), 581–587.

Knowles, G., Sherony, K., & Haupert, M. (1992). The demand for major league baseball: A test of the uncertainty of outcome hypothesis. *American Economist, 36*(2), 72–80.

Koch, K. (1895). *Die Geschichte des Fußballs im Altertum und in der Neuzeit.* Berlin: Gärtners Verlagsbuchhandlung.

Konietzka, D. & Kreyenfeld, M. (2002). Women's employment and non-marital childbearing: A comparison between East and West Germany in the 1990s. *Population, 57*(2), 331–357.

Konjer, M., Meier, H. E., & Wedeking, K. (2017). Consumer demand for telecasts of tennis matches in Germany. *Journal of Sports Economics, 18*(4), 351–375.

Konjer, M., Mutz, M., & Meier, H. E. (2019). Talent alone does not suffice: Erotic capital, media visibility and global popularity among professional male and female tennis players. *Journal of Gender Studies, 28*(1), 3–17.

Krane, V., Ross, S. R., Miller, M., Rowse, J. L., Ganoe, K., Andrzejczyk, J. A., & Lucas, C. B. (2010). Power and focus: Self-representation of female college athletes. *Qualitative Research in Sport and Exercise, 2*(2), 175–195.

Krebs, H. D. (1995). Die politische Instrumentalisierung des Sports in der DDR. In *Materialien der Enquete Kommission. Aufarbeitung von Geschichte und Folgen der SED Diktatur in Deutschland des Deutschen Bundestages* (pp. 1315–1369). Berlin: Deutscher Bundestag.

Krüger, M. (1996). Body culture and nation building: The history of gymnastics in germany in the period of its foundation as a nation-state. *The international Journal of the History of Sport, 13*(3), 409–417.

Küchenmeister, D. & Schneider, T. (2014). Die Frauenfußball-Weltmeisterschaft 2011—ein kritischer Rückblick auf gesellschaft spolitische Debatten. In A. R. Hofmann & M. Krüger (eds), *Rund um den Frauenfußball: Pädagogische und sozialwissenschaftliche Perspektiven* (pp. 63–67). Münster: Waxmann.

Kuypers, T. (1996). The beautiful game? An econometric study of why people watch English football. Discussion Paper No. 96 (01). University College London, Department of Economics.

Lagaert, S. & Roose, H. (2018). The gender gap in sport event attendance in Europe: The impact of macro-level gender equality. *International Review for the Sociology of Sport, 53*(5), 533–549.

Langewiesche, D. (1990). '… für Volk und Vaterland kräftig zu würken …': Zur politischen und gesellschaftlichen Rolle der Turner zwischen 1811 und 1871. In O. Gruppe (ed.), *Körperkult oder Kulturgut? Sport und Sportwissenschaft im Wandel* (pp. 22–61). Tübingen: Attempto.

140 *References*

Lee, K. S., Alwin, D. F. & Tufis, P. A. (2007). Beliefs about women's labour in the reunified Germany, 1991–2004. *European Sociological Review, 23*(4), 487–503.

Lee, Y. H. & Fort, R. D. (2008). Attendance and the uncertainty of outcome hypothesis in Baseball. *Review of Industrial Organisation, 33*(4), 281–295.

Leeds, E. M. & Leeds, M. A. (2012). Gold, silver, and bronze: Determining national success in men's and women's Summer Olympic events. *Jahrbücher für Nationalökonomie und Statistik, 232*(3), 279–292.

LeFeuvre, A. D., Stephenson, E. F., & Walcott, S. M. (2013). Football frenzy: The effect of the 2011 World Cup on women's professional league attendance. *Journal of Sports Economics, 14*(4), 440–448.

Leibert, T. (2016). She leaves, he stays? Sex-selective migration in rural East Germany. *Journal of Rural Studies, 43*, 267–279.

Leibert, T. & Golinski, S. (2017). Peripheralisation: The missing link in dealing with demographic change? *Comparative Population Studies, 41*(3–4), 1–30.

Leibert, T. & Wiest, K. (2016). The interplay of gender and migration in Europe's remote and economically weak rural regions: Introduction to a special issue. *Journal of Rural Studies, 100*(43), 261–266.

Linne, C. S. (2011). *Frei gespielt: Frauenfußball im geteilten Deutschland.* Berlin: Bebra.

Linne, C. S. (2014). Der vergessene Osten? Die Entwicklung des Frauenfußballs in der DDR und seine Bedeutung für den vereinten Spielbetrieb. In S. Sinning, J. Pargätzi, & B. Eichmann (eds), *Frauen-und Mädchenfußball im Blickpunkt: Empirische Untersuchungen-Probleme und Visionen* (pp. 13–28). Berlin: LIT Verlag.

Liston, K. (2006). Sport and gender relations. *Sport in Society, 9*(4), 616–633.

Lopez, S. (1997). *Women on the Ball: a Guide to Women's Football.* London: Scarlet Press.

Lowen, A., Deaner, R. O., & Schmitt, E. (2016). Guys and gals going for gold: The role of women's empowerment in Olympic success. *Journal of Sports Economics, 17*(3), 260–285.

Luh, A. (2003). On the way to a national socialist sports system: From liberal sports in clubs and associations to directed sports in national socialist organizations. *European Journal of Sport Science, 3*(3), 1–10.

Magowan, A. (2019). What is the state of women's football attendances after recent records? April 19. Available at: www.bbc.com/sport/football/47871431.

Manzenreiter, W. (2008). The 'benefits' of hosting: Japanese experiences from the 2002 Football World Cup. *Asian Business & Management, 7*(2), 201–224.

Manzenreiter, W. & Horne, J. (2007). Playing the post-fordist game in/to the Far East: The footballisation of China, Japan and South Korea. *Soccer & Society, 8*(4), 561–577.

Mau, S. (2004). Welfare regimes and the norms of social exchange. *Current Sociology, 52*(1), 53–74.

McCabe, C. (2007). Spectators' attitudes toward basketball: An application of multifactorial gender identity. *North American Journal of Psychology, 9*(2), 211–228.

References 141

McCabe, C. (2008). Gender effects on spectators' attitudes toward WNBA Basketball. *Social Behavior and Personality, 36*(3), 347–358.

McPherson, M. (1983). An ecology of affiliation. *American Sociological Review, 48*(4), 519–532.

Meier, H. E. (2004). Solidarität und Marktmacht: Die politische Regulierung der Zentralvermarktung der Fußball-Bundesliga. *Sport und Gesellschaft, 1*(2), 125–144.

Meier, H. E. & Hagenah, J. (2016). 'Fußballisierung' im deutschen Fernsehen? Eine Intersuchung zum Wandel von Angebot und Nachfrage bei den wichtigsten Free TV-Sendern. *M&K Medien & Kommunikationswissenscha ft, 64*(1), 12–35.

Meier, H. E. & Leinwather, M. (2012). Women as 'armchair audience'? Evidence from German national team football. *Sociology of Sport Journal, 29*(3), 365–384.

Meier, H. E. & Leinwather, M. (2013). Finally a 'taste for diversity'? National identity, consumer discrimination, and the multi-ethnic German National Football Team. *European Sociological Review, 29*(6), 1201–1213.

Meier, H. E. & Mutz, M. (2016). Sport-related national pride in East and West Germany, 1992–2008: Persistent differences or trends toward convergence? *Sage Open, 6*(3). Available at: https://journals.sagepub.com/doi/pdf/10.1177/2158244016665893.

Meier, H. E., Konjer, M., & Leinwather, M. (2016). The demand for women's league soccer in Germany. *European Sport Management Quarterly, 16*(1), 1–19.

Meier, H. E., Konjer, M., & Nagm, A. (2017). The spatial restructuring of competitive tennis in Germany. *German Journal of Exercise and Sport Research, 47*(3), 205–220.

Meier, H. E., Reinhart, K., Konjer, M., & Leinwather, M. (2016). Deutschland, einig Fußballland? Ost-West-Unterschiede in der Nachfrage nach Nationalmannschaftsspielen. *Leviathan, 44*(2), 247–279.

Meier, H. E., Strauß, B., & Riedl, D. (2017). Feminization of sport audiences and fans? Evidence from the German men's national soccer team. *International Review for the Sociology of Sport, 52*(6), 712–733.

Melzer, M. & Stäglin, R. (1965). Zur Ökonomie des Fußballs: Eine empirischtheoretische Analyse der Bundesliga. *Konjunkturpolitik, 11*, 114–137.

Messner, M. (1992). *Power at play: Sports and the Problem of Masculinity.* Boston, MA: Beacon Press.

Meuren, D. (2015). Ein Blick in die Zukunft des Frauenfußballs: Sieben Millionen Fernsehzuschauer bei der WM zeigen die Attraktivität des Nationalteams. *Frankfurter Allgemeine Zeitung*, June 14, p. 36.

Meuren, D. (2018). Frauen im Schatten: Der deutsche Frauenfußball hatte einst eine Vorreiterrolle, jetzt droht er in der zweiten Reihe zu verschwinden. Die WM-Qualifikation auf Island gilt als Schlüsselspiel für die Zukunft. *Frankfurter Allgemeine Zeitung*, September 1, p. 36.

Meuren, D. (2019). 'Das Feld hat uns links und rechts überholt': Siegfried Dietrich, Sprecher der Frauen-Bundesliga über das frühe WM-Aus, die

142 References

Reaktionen des DFB und den Vorsprung der Amerikanerinnen. *Frankfurter Allgemeine Zeitung*, July 8, p. 25.

Minkus, L. & Busch-Heimann, A. (2018). Gender wage inequalities between historical heritage and structural adjustments: A German–German comparison over time. *Social Politics: International Studies in Gender, State & Society, 0*(0), 1–31.

Mongeon, K. & Winfree, J. (2012). Comparison of television and gate demand in the National Basketball Association. *Sport Management Review, 15*(1), 72–79.

Müller, K. U., Neumann, M., & Wrohlich, K. (2018). The family working-time model: Towards more gender equality in work and care. *Journal of European Social Policy, 28*(5), 471–486.

Neale, W. C. (1964). The peculiar economics of professional sports: A contribution to the theory of the firm in sporting competition and in market competition. *Quarterly Journal of Economics, 78*(1), 1–14.

Nieland, J.-U. (2013). Weltmeisterschaften als Sprungbretter der medialen Wahrnehmung des Frauenfußballs? Die Berichterstattung in deutschen Printmedien im Zeitverlauf. In M. Herzog (ed.), *Frauenfußball in Deutschland: Anfänge—Verbote—Widerstände—Durchbruch* (pp. 241–262). Stuttgart: Kohlhammer.

Noland, M. & Stahler, K. (2016). What goes into a medal: Women's inclusion and success at the Olympic Games. *Social Science Quarterly, 97*(2), 177–196.

Nüesch, S. & Franck, E. (2009). The role of patriotism in explaining the TV audience of national team games: Evidence from four international tournaments. *Journal of Media Economics, 22*(1), 6–19.

Oncescu, J. (2015). Rural restructuring and its impact on community recreation opportunities. *Annals of Leisure Research, 18*(1), 83–104.

Oncescu, J. & Robertson, B. (2010). Recreation in remote communities: A case study of a Nova Scotia Village. *Journal of Rural and Community Development, 5*(1): 221–237.

O'Reilly, N., Berger, I. E., Hernandez, T., Parent, M. M., & Séguin, B. (2015). Urban sportscapes: An environmental deterministic perspective on the management of youth sport participation. *Sport Management Review, 18*(2), 291–307.

Oswald, R. (2008). *Fußball-Volksgemeinschaft: Ideologie, Politik und Fanatismus im deutschen Fußball 1919–1964*. Frankfurt am Main: Campus.

Pan, W. (2001). Akaike's information criterion in generalized estimating equations. *Biometrics, 57*(1), 120–125.

Paul, R. J. & Weinbach, A. P. (2007). The uncertainty of outcome and scoring effects on Nielsen ratings for Monday Night Football. *Journal of Economics and Business, 59*(3), 199–211.

Pawlowski, T. (2013). Testing the uncertainty of outcome hypothesis in European professional football: A stated preference approach. *Journal of Sports Economics, 14*(4), 341–367.

References 143

Pawlowski, T. & Anders, C. (2012). Stadium attendance in German professional football: The (un)importance of uncertainty of outcome reconsidered. *Applied Economics Letters, 19*(6), 1553–1556.

Pawlowski, T., Breuer, C., & Hovemann, A. (2010). Top clubs' performance and the competitive situation in European domestic football competitions. *Journal of Sports Economics, 11*(2), 186–202.

Peel, D. A. & Thomas, D. A. (1992). The demand for football: Some evidence on outcome uncertainty. *Empirical Economics, 17*(2), 323–331.

Pelak, C. F. (2010). Women and gender in South African soccer: A brief history. *Soccer & Society, 11*(1–2), 63–78.

Pfister, G. (ed.) (1980). *Frau und Sport*. Frankfurt am Main: Fischer.

Pfister, G. (1993). 'Der Kampf gebührt dem Mann …': Argumente und gegenargumente im diskurs über den frauensport. In R. Renson (ed.), *Sport and Contest* (pp. 349–365). Madrid: INEF.

Pfister, G. (2001). 'Must women play football?' Women's football in Germany, past and present. *Football Studies, 4*(2), 41–57.

Pfister, G. (2002). *Frauen und Sport in der DDR*. Köln: Buch + Sport Strauß.

Pfister, G. (2003). The challenges of women's football in East and West Germany: A comparative study. *Soccer & Society, 4*(2–3), 128–148.

Pfister, G. (2006). The future of football is female!? On the past and present of women's football in Germany. In A. Tomlinson & C. Young (eds), *German Football: History, Culture, Society* (pp. 93–126). London: Routledge.

Pfister, G. 2008. Doing sport is doing gender. *Beiträge zur feministischen Theorie und Praxis, 60*(31), 13–30.

Pierson, P. (1993). When effect becomes cause: Policy feedback and political change. *World Politics, 45*(4), 595–628.

Politbüro des Zentralkomitees (1998 [1969]). Anlage Nr. 3 zum Protokoll Nr. 15 vom 8. 4. 1969: Die weitere Entwicklung des Leistungssports bis zu den Olympischen Spielen 1972. In G. Spitzer, H.J. Teichler & K. Reinartz (eds), *Schlüsseldokumente zum DDR-Sport: Ein Sporthistorischer Überblick in Originalquellen* (pp. 154–174). Meyer & Meyer: Aachen.

Pollmann-Schult, M. & Reynolds, J. (2017). The work and wishes of fathers: Actual and preferred work hours among German fathers. *European Sociological Review, 33*(6), 823–838.

Rabe-Hesketh, S. & Skrondal, A. (2012). *Multilevel and Longitudinal Modeling using Stata*. College Station, TX: Stata Press.

Regionalstatistik. (2014a). Tabelle 426-71-4: Bruttoinlandsprodukt/ Bruttowertschöpfung (WZ 2008)—Jahressumme—regionale Tiefe: Kreise und kreisfreie Städte. Available at: www. regionalstatistik.de/genesis/ online/data;jsessionid=A3B3C1BB28B499A5B30C58A22291519A?opera tion=abruftabelleAbrufen&selectionname=426-71-4&levelindex=1&leve lid=14048875577 53&index=4.

Regionalstatistik. (2014b). Tabelle 666-51-4: Verfügbares Einkommen der privaten Haushalte einschließlich privater Organisationen ohne Erwerbszweck—Jahressumme—regionale Tiefe: Kreise und kreisfreie

144   References

Städte. Available at: www.regionalstatistik.de/genesis/online/data;jsessionid
=49C950C417E47CD2E30A0F9FA3C135AC?operation=abruftabelleAbr
ufen&selectionname=666-51-4&levelindex=1&levelid=1404888025758&in
dex=3.

Reinartz, K. (1999). Die Zweiteilung des DDR-Sports auf Beschluss der SED.
In H. J. Teichler & K. Reinartz (eds), *Das Leistungssportsystem der DDR in
den 80er Jahren und im Prozeß der Wende* (pp. 55–86). Schorndorf: Hofmann.

Rich, T. (2013). Relegation scandal takes toll on Doncaster Rovers Belles.
Available at: www.independent.co.uk/sport/football/news-and-comment/
relegation-scandal-takes-toll-on-doncaster-rovers-belles-8650856.html.

Rosenfeld, R. A., Trappe, H. & Gornick, J. C. (2004). Gender and work in
Germany: Before and after reunification. *Annual Review of Sociology, 30*,
103–124.

Rosso, E. (2008). The spatial organisation of women's soccer in Adelaide:
Another tale of spatial inequality? *Geographical Research, 46*(4), 446–458.

Rottenberg, S. (1956). The baseball players' labor-market. *Journal of Political
Economy, 64*, 242–258.

Rottmann, H. & Seitz, F. (2008). Wer und was bestimmen die Zuschauerzahlen
in der Fußballbundesliga? Schmollers Jahrbuch. *Zeitschrift für Wirtschafts-
und Sozialwissenschaften, 128*(2), 291–306.

Rulofs, B. & Hartmann-Tews, I. (2011). Geschlechterverhältnisse in der
medialen Vermittlung von Sport: Sexualisierung und Erotisierung als
Inszenierungsstrategien. In D. Schaaf and J.-U. Nieland (eds), *Die
Sexualisierung des Sports in den Medien* (pp. 100–113). Köln: Halem.

Schaaf, D. (2013). Vom Mannweib zur sexy Kickerin: Veränderungen und
Kontinuitäten im redaktionellen Auswahlprozess des Frauenfußballs.
In M. Herzog (ed.), *Frauenfußball in Deutschland: Anfänge—Verbote—
Widerstände—Durchbruch* (pp. 263–284). Stuttgart: Kohlhammer.

Schaaf, D. (2014). Gefangen im Klischee? Mediale Inszenierung von
Weiblichkeit im Frauenfußball. In A.R. Hoffmann & M. Krüger (eds), *Rund
um den Frauenfußball: Pädagogische und Sozialwissenschaftliche Perspektiven*
(pp. 30–79). Münster: Waxmann.

Schröder, B. (2017). *Ein Trainerleben für den Frauenfußball.* Berlin: Steffen
Verlag.

Scraton, S., Fasting, K., Pfister, G., & Bunuel, A. (1999). It's still a man's game?
The experiences of top-level European women footballers. *International
Review for the Sociology of Sport, 34*(2), 99–111.

Selmer, N. (2004). *Watching the Boys Play: Frauen als Fußballfans.* Kassel:
Agon-Sportverlag.

Sfeir, L. (1985). The status of Muslim women in sport: Conflict between cultural tradition and modernization. *International Review for the Sociology of
Sport, 20*(4), 283–306.

Shildrick, T. (2006). Youth culture, subculture and the importance of neigh-
bourhood. *Young, 14*(1), 61–74.

Shildrick, T. & MacDonald, R. (2006). In defence of subculture: Young people,
leisure and social divisions. *Journal of Youth Studies, 9*(2), 125–140.

References 145

Simmons, R. (1996). The demand for English league football: A club-level analysis. *Applied Economics, 28*(2), 139–155.

Simmons, R. (2006). The demand for spectator sports. In W. Andreff, & S. Szymanski (eds), *Handbook on the Economics of Sport* (pp. 77–89). Cheltenham: Edward Elgar.

Sinn, G. & Sinn, H. W. (1992). *Kaltstart. Volkswirtschaftliche Aspekte der deutschen Vereinigung*. Tübingen: Monograph, Mohr Siebeck.

Sloan, L. R. (1989). The motives of sports fans. In J. H. Goldstein (ed.), *Sports Games and Play: Social and Psychological Viewpoints* (pp. 175–240). Hillsdale, NJ: Lawrence Erlbaum Associates.

Snower, D. J. & Merkl, C. (2006). The caring hand that cripples: The East German labor market after reunification. *American Economic Review, 96*(2), 375–382.

Solberg, H. A. (2002). The economics of television sports rights. Europe and the US: A comparative analysis. *Norsk Medietidsskrift, 9*(2), 57–80.

Soss, J. & Schram, S. F. (2007). A public transformed? Welfare reform as policy feedback. *American Political Science Review, 101*(1), 111–127.

Staab, M. (2017). Erlebte Geschichte: Die Anfänge des Frauenfußballs nach 1970. In G. Sobiech & S. Günter (eds), *Sport & Gender: (Inter)nationale Sportsoziologische Geschlechterforschung* (pp. 49–58). Wiesbaden: Springer Fachmedien.

Statistisches Bundesamt (2013). *Zensus 2011: 80,2 Millionen Einwohner lebten am 9. Mai 2011 in Deutschland. Rund 1,5 Millionen Einwohner weniger als bislang angenommen*. Available at: www.presseportal.de/pm/32102/2482995 (accessed December 28, 2019).

Statistisches Bundesamt [Federal Statistical Office]. (2018). *Verbraucherpreisindex*. Available at: www.destatis.de/DE/ZahlenFakten/Indikatoren/Konjunkturindi katoren/Preise/pre110.html;jsessionid=FFAD359285385144B23E36D7A50 802DB.InternetLive1.

Stigler, G. J. & Becker, G. S. (1977). De gustibus non est disputandum. *American Economic Review, 67*(2), 76–90.

Stroth, S. (2018). *Gender differences in TV viewership in German boxing audiences*. Unpublished Master's thesis, University of Münster.

Svallfors, S. (1997). Worlds of welfare and attitudes to redistribution: A comparison of eight Western nations. *European Sociological Review, 13*(3), 283–304.

Svallfors, S. (2006). *The Moral Economy of Class: Class and Attitudes in Comparative Perspective*. Stanford, CA: Stanford University Press.

Svallfors, S. (2010). Policy feedback, generational replacement, and attitudes to state intervention: Eastern and Western Germany, 1990–2006. *European Political Science Review, 2*(1), 119–135.

Szymanski, S. (2003). The economic design of sporting contests. *Journal of Economic Literature, 41*, 1137–1187.

Szymanski, S. (2014). Insolvency in English football. In J. Goddard & P. Sloane (eds), *Handbook on the Economics of Professional Football* (pp. 100–116). Cheltenham: Edward Elgar.

146 References

Tagesspiegel (2017). Norwegens Fußballfrauen verdienen bald so viel wie die Männer. Available at: www.tagesspiegel.de/sport/lohngleichheit-im-fussball-norwegens-fussballfrauen-verdienen-bald-so-viel-wie-die-maenner/20433914.html.

Tainsky, S. (2010). Television broadcast demand for National Football League contests. *Journal of Sports Economics, 11*(6), 629–640.

Tainsky, S. & McEvoy, C. D. (2012). Television broadcast demand in markets without local teams. *Journal of Sports Economics, 13*(3), 250–265.

Tainsky, S. & Winfree, J. A. (2010). Short-run demand and uncertainty of outcome in Major League Baseball. *Review of Industrial Organization, 37*(3), 197–214.

Tate, T. (2013). *Girls with Balls: The Secret History of Women's Football.* London: John Blake Publishing.

Tcha, M. & Pershin, V. (2003). Reconsidering performance at the Summer Olympics and revealed comparative advantage. *Journal of Sports Economics, 4*(3), 216–239.

Tegelbeckers, L. W. (2003). SG-Sport im Spiegel von Plan und 'Erfüllung': Eine regionale Studie zu Proportionen und Disproportionen im DTSB-organisierten Basissport. In H. J. Teichler (ed.), *Sport in der DDR: Eigensinn, Konflikte, Trends* (pp. 135–235). Köln, Germany: Sport und Buch Strauß.

Teichler, H. J. (2002). *Die Sportbeschlüsse des Politbüros: Eine Studie zum Verhältnis von SED und Sport mit einem Gesamtverzeichnis und einer Dokumentation ausgewählter Beschlüsse.* Köln: Sport und Buch Strauss.

Tonts, M. (2005). Competitive sport and social capital in rural Australia. *Journal of Rural Studies, 21*(2), 137–149.

Tonts, M. & Atherley, K. (2005). Rural restructuring and the changing geography of competitive sport. *Australian Geographer, 36*(2), 125–144.

Torgler, B. (2008). The determinants of women's international soccer performances. *International Journal of Sport Management and Marketing, 3*(4), 305–318.

Trail, G. T., Anderson, D. F., & Fink, J. S. (2002). Examination of gender differences in importance of and satisfaction with venue factors at intercollegiate basketball games. *International Sports Journal, 6*(1), 51–64.

Trappe, H. & Rosenfeld, R. A. (2000). How do children matter? A comparison of gender earnings inequality for young adults in the former East Germany and the former West Germany. *Journal of Marriage and Family, 62*(2), 489–507.

Trappe, H., Pollmann-Schult, M., & Schmitt, C. (2015). The rise and decline of the male breadwinner model: Institutional underpinnings and future expectations. *European Sociological Review, 31*(2), 230–242.

Trivedi, P. & Zimmer, D. (2014). Success at the Summer Olympics: How much do economic factors explain? *Econometrics, 2*(4), 169–202.

Uhlig, H. (2008). The slow decline of East Germany. *Journal of Comparative Economics, 36*(4), 517–541.

UNDP (2018). *Human Development Data (1990–2015).* Available at: http://hdr.undp.org/en/data.

References   147

UNESCO (2011). *Human Development Report 2011*. New York: Palgrave Macmillan.

Valenti, M., Scelles, N., & Morrow, S. (2018). Women's football studies: An integrative review. *Sport, Business and Management: An International Journal, 8*(5), 511–528.

Van Ingen, C. (2003). Geographies of gender, sexuality and race: Reframing the focus on space in sport sociology. *International Review for the Sociology of Sport, 38*(2), 201–216.

Vaupel, C. (2014). Gelingt es dem DFB mit seinen konzeptionellen Programmen (speziell: DFB TEAM 2011-Kampagne) mehr Mädchen für den Fußball zu begeistern? In S. Sinning, J. Pargätzi & B. Eichmann (eds), *Frauen- und Mädchenfußball im Blickpunkt: Empirische Untersuchungen—Probleme und Visionen* (pp. 187–200). Münster: Lit.

Vincent, J., Pedersen, P. M., Whisenant, W. A., & Massey, D. (2007). Analysing the print media coverage of professional tennis players: British newspaper narratives about female competitors in the Wimbledon Championships. *International Journal of Sport Management and Marketing, 2*(3), 281–300.

Walter, J. G. (2018). The adequacy of measures of gender roles attitudes: A review of current measures in omnibus surveys. *Quality & Quantity, 52*(2), 829–848.

Wann, D. L. & Waddill, P. J. (2003). Predicting sport fan motivation using anatomical sex and gender role orientation. *North American Journal of Psychology, 5*(3), 485–498.

Welki, A. A. & Zlatoper, T. J. (1994). US professional football: The demand for game-day attendance in 1991. *Managerial and Decision Economics, 15*(5), 489–495.

Whiteside, E. & Hardin, M. (2011). Women (not) watching women: Leisure time, television, and implications for televised coverage of women's sports. *Communication, Culture and Critique, 4*(2), 122–143.

Wicker, P. & Frick, B. (2015). The relationship between intensity and duration of physical activity and subjective well-being. *The European Journal of Public Health*, 25(5), 868–872.

Wicker, P., Breuer, C., & Pawlowski, T. (2009). Promoting sport for all to age-specific target groups: The impact of sport infrastructure. *European Sport Management Quarterly, 9*(2), 103–118.

Wiechmann, T. & Pallagst, K. M. (2012). Urban shrinkage in Germany and the USA: A comparison of transformation patterns and local strategies. *International Journal of Urban and Regional Research, 36*(2), 261–280.

Williams, J. (2003). The fastest growing sport? Women's football in England. *Soccer & Society, 4*(2–3), 112–127.

Williams, J. (2013). *A Game for Rough Girls? A History of Women's Football in Britain*. London: Routledge.

Williams, J. (2014). *A Contemporary History of Women's Sport, Part One: Sporting Women, 1850–1960*. London: Routledge.

148 References

Williamson, L. (2013). Manchester City cash muscles into ladies' game as Doncaster Belles are booted out of league (even if they finish top!). Available at: www.dailymail.co.uk/sport/football/article-2340843/Doncaster-Rovers-Belles-relegated-make-way-Manchester-City.html.

Witte, J. C. & Wagner, G. G. (1995). Employment and fertility in East Germany after unification. Discussion Papers 125, DIW Berlin, German Institute for Economic Research.

Wopp, C. (2007). Zukunftsfaktor Frauenfußball. In G. Gdawietz & U. Kraus (eds), *Die Zukunft des Fußballs ist weiblich. Beiträge zum Frauen-und Mädchenfußball* (pp. 9–32). Aachen: Meyer & Meyer.

ZDFsport (2013). Da sind sie, die Damen Fußballerinnen! Available at: www.youtube.com/watch?v=SidwRv9hhPQ.

Zoch, G. & Schober, P. S. (2018). Public child-care expansion and changing gender ideologies of parents in Germany. *Journal of Marriage and Family, 80*(4), 1020–1039.

Zubayr, C. & Gerhard, H. (2005). Tendenzen im Zuschauerverhalten. *Media Perspektiven, 2005*(3), 94–104.

Zubayr, C. & Gerhard, H. (2011). Tendenzen im Zuschauerverhalten: Fernsehgewohnheiten und Fernsehreichweiten im Jahr 2010. *Media Perspektiven, 2011*(3), 126–138.

Zubayr, C. & Gerhard, H. (2017). Tendenzen im Zuschauerverhalten: Fernsehgewohnheiten und Fernsehreichweiten im Jahr 2016. *Media Perspektiven, 2017*(3), 130–144.

Index

Note: References to tables are in **bold**; references to figures are in *italics*

1. FC Köln **56**, 57
1. FFC Frankfurt **56**

A Juniors 31, *32*, **40**, 41, **42**, 43
affiliation of teams, in Frauen-
  Bundesliga 56–7, **56**, **61**, 64, **66**,
  69–70, **117**
Afghanistan, Gender Inequality
  Value (GIV) 2, *2*
Akerlof, G.A. 23
Aktuelles Sportstudio 72
Algarve Cup (2014) 79
Anders, C. 51, 52, 53, 54, 112
Atherley, K. 26
ATSB (Workers' Gymnastic and
  Sport Association) 11
attendance levels *see* stadium
  attendance
audiences *see* stadium attendance;
  TV ratings/coverage

B Juniors 31, *32*, **40**, **42**
Bale, J. 21
banning of women's soccer 10, 11,
  12–13
Bavaria 34, **34**, **37**, 39, **40**, 41, **43**, 99
Bayer 04 Leverkusen 50
Bayern Munich 50
Beckenbauer, Franz 50
Benz, M.-A. 54
Blatter, Sepp 1
Borland, J. 51
Brandenburg 32, **34**, 35, **37**, **40**, 41, **43**
Brandes, L. 53, 54

Breuer, M. 52
BSG (company sports associations)
  15, 20–1, 26–7
Büch, M.-P. 54
Buraimo, B. 54
Buytendijk, F.J.J. 12

C Juniors 31, *32*, **40**, **42**
childcare 7, 8, 9
Cho, S.Y. 4
communism *see* East Germany
company sports associations (BSG)
  15, 20–1, 26–7
Congdon-Hohman, J. 4, 5
consumer loyalty 51, 55, **61**, 64, **66**,
  69, 76
Czarnitzki, D. 51, 52, 53, 54

D Juniors 31, *32*, **40**, **42**
DFB (Deutscher Fußballbund):
  banning of women's soccer 11,
  12–13; creation of national league
  47–8; creation of women's national
  team 13; data from 104–5; feminine
  image of soccer 72–3; programs for
  promotion of women's soccer 14,
  20, 72–3
Dobson, S.M. 51
Doncaster Belles (England) 50

E Juniors 31, *32*, **40**, **42**
East Germany: economy of 23;
  gender policies 7–8, 75–6; grass-
  roots soccer 15, 20–1, 25–7, 31–2,

150   *Index*

34, **34**, 35, *35*, **37**, 39, **40**, 41, **43**, 44, 45, 99; impact of reunification 23–4; legacies from 6, 16, 25–8, 30, 39, 44, 45, 97–9; national soccer team 6, 76, 92; national women's league 47; and out-migration 22–3, 24–5, 26, 27–8, 35, 44, 99; priority of the Olympics 14–15; and reunification 6, 8, 9, 16, 20, 23–4, 26, 27; rural restructuring 22–4, 26, 27–8, 44, 99; sport-centered identity politics 6; TV ratings/ coverage 78, 80, *80*, **81–2**, **85–7**, 88–9, *88–9*, 92; women's soccer in (overview) 14–17, 26–7, 98
Empor Dresden 21
English Football Association (FA) 10, 50
eroticized marketing 73
EURO tournaments (UEFA) **62**, **63**, 65, **67**, 71, 72, 74, 77, **81**, **85**, **118**, 121, **123**
European Competition for Women's Football (1989) 13, 72

F Juniors 31, *32*, **40**, 41, **42**, 43
family labor 7–9
fan loyalty 51, 55, **61**, 64, **66**, 69, 76
FBL *see* Frauen-Bundesliga (FBL)
FC Eintracht Rheine **56**
FCR 2001 Duisburg **56**
FCR Duisburg **56**
fertility rates 3, 10, 11, 23
FFC Brauweiler Pulheim 2000 **56**, 56–7
FFC Heike Rheine 48, **56**
FIFA: attitude to women's soccer 1; impact of programs 4; rankings of women's national soccer teams *2*, 77–8, 103, **104**
FIFA World Cups *see* World Cups
first-tier league soccer *see* Frauen-Bundesliga (FBL)
Forrest, D. 59, 115
Fortuna Düsseldorf 12
Franck, E. 53, 54
Frauen-Bundesliga (FBL) 47–70; analysis of attendance data 55–9, **56**, *58*; attendance levels 59–69, *60*, **61–3**, **66–8**; competitive imbalance

48, *49*; and consumer loyalty 51, 55, **61**, 64, **66**, 69, 76; data sources/ datasets 112–19; determinants of stadium attendance 51–5; and displacement 50; early development of 47–8; media attention 48; and national team success 59, **61**, 64–5, **66**, 70, 115, **116**; as niche product 51, 55, 59, 69, 70; resources for 50; semi-professional status 48; subsidization by men's clubs 48, 50, 56–7, 70, 100; team affiliations 56–7, **56**, **61**, 64, **66**, 69–70, **117**; team survival 48, *49*, 107–8
free-to-air TV 71, 78, 122
Frick, B. 51, 54
future for women's soccer 96–7
future research 100–1

G Juniors 31, *32*, **40**, **42**
Gärtner, M. 52, 53, 54
GDP and soccer team performance **5**, 5–6
gender, and sport spectatorship *80*, **81–7**, *88–9*, 90–1, 92–3, **123**, **127–9**
gender equality/inequality: before and after reunification 7–9, 75–6; and development of women's soccer 9–17; and growth of women's soccer 92–3, 96–9; measuring 1–2, *2*, 3, **5**, 103; media bias 93; pay gap 3–4, 7, 8, 9; and soccer team performance 1–3, *2*, 3–6, **5**; and sporting success 3
Gender Inequality Value (GIV) 1–2, *2*, 3, **5**, 103
gender pay gap 3–4, 7, 8, 9
gender policies, before and after reunification 7–9, 75
gender roles: East Germany 7–8; and English FA banning of soccer 10; under Hitler 11; modernization of attitudes 74–6; the 'new woman' 11; and outmigration 24–5; and sport spectatorship 92–3; West Germany 7, 9, 12, 14
German Empire 10–11
Germany (general): development of women's soccer 9–17; Gender Inequality Value (GIV) 2, *2*;

gender policies before and after reunification 7–9; as ideal case study 6; labor force participation 9; reunification of 6, 8, 9, 16
Goddard, J.A. 51
grass-roots soccer 20–46; data analysis 28–31, *29*, 111; data sources and dataset 104–11; in East Germany 15, 20–1, 25–7, 31–2, 34, **34**, 35, *35*, **37**, 39, **40**, 41, **43**, 44, 45, 99; East-West divide 23–5, 26, 28, 34–5, 39, 44; impact of macro-social conditions 22–5, **36–8**, 39, **42**, 44–5; impact of meso-level factors 44–6; infrastructure 22–3; institutional legacies 25–8, 44, 45; key role of sports organizations 99; as spatially constrained activities 21–2, 44–5; stagnation and regional diversity 31–43, *32–3*, **34**, *35*, **36–8**, **40–3**; team survival 30, 31, **34**, 34, *35*, 39–43, **40–3**, 44, 45–6, 107–8; in West Germany 13, 20, 26, **34**, 35, *35*, **37–8**, 39, **40–1**, 41, **43**, 44, 45, 99
Grün-Weiß Brauweiler **56**
gymnastics (Turnen) movement 10, 11

Hannan, M.T. 24
Hardin, J.W. 111, 127
Hardin, M. 93
health, and sport 10, 11, 12
Hennies, R. 15, 48, 68
Herzog, M. 13
Hesse **34**, **37**, 39, **40**, 41, **43**
Hilbe, J.M. 111, 127
Hitler, Adolf 11
Hoffmann, R. 3–4
Hoggart, K. 22
host site characteristics and stadium attendance 51, 57, 59, **61**, 64, 65, **66**, 69, 114, 119
Hutchins, B. 91

institutional legacies 6–7, 16, 17, 45, 97–8; impact on grassroots soccer in East Germany 25–8, 30, 39, 44, 45, 97–8
interpretive effects of policies 16, 17, 25, 26, 27, 98

Islam 3, 4

Jacobs, J.C. 4, 101
Janssens, P. 55, 112

Késenne, S. 55, 112
Klein, M.W. 3
Konjer, M. 30, 112

labor force participation 3, 4, 7–8, 9, 75
Lagaert, S. 97
Leeds, E.M. 3
Leeds, M.A. 3
LeFeuvre, A.D. 59
Leinwather, M. 72, 112
liberal-feminist discourse 18
Lowen, A. 3
Lower Saxony 32, 34, **34**, **37**, **40**, **43**, 45, 99
loyalty of fans 51, 55, **61**, 64, **66**, 69, 76

Macdonald, R. 51
male breadwinner model 7, 8, 9, 75
Manchester City 50
marketing of women's soccer 59, 70, 73, 99
masculine hegemony 9–11, 12–14, 93
Matheson, V.A. 4, 5
McCabe, C. 74
McPherson, M. 24
Mecklenburg-West Pomerania 32, **34**, **37**, **40**, 41, **43**
media attention: commercial entrepreneurs 12; eroticized marketing 73; Frauen-Bundesliga 48, 59; negative attitudes 71–2; *see also* TV ratings/coverage
Melzer, M. 53
men's league clubs: fielding women's teams 48, 50, 56–7, 70, 100; stadium attendance 54, 59–60
men's national soccer team: determinants of performance 4; national icon status 71; Nazi portrayal of 11; popularity in East Germany 6; World Cup 1954 12, 71; TV coverage 71, 72

152 Index

men's soccer (general): stadium attendance 51, 52–4
men's TV viewing habits *80*, **81–7**, *88–9*, 90–1, 92–3, **123**, **127–9**
Meuren, D. 15, 48, 68
Middle Rhine **34**, **37**, **40**, **43**
militarism 10
motherhood 7–8, 9, 75

national soccer team 71–93; data sources/ dataset 119–25; dataset modeling approach 126–9; DFB campaigns 72–3; dominance of 73–4; East German interest in 6, 76, 92; FIFA ranking of *2*, 77–8, 103, 104; and modernization of gender-role attitudes 74–6; policy legacies 92; professionalization of 74; TV coverage/ratings 71–2, 76–92, *79–80*, **81–7**, *88–9*, 99; *see also* EURO tournaments; World Cups
national women's league *see* Frauen-Bundesliga (FBL)
Nazis 11–12
'new woman' 11
Noland, M. 3

Olympic Games 3, 14–15, 27, **63**, **68**, 77, **81**, **85**
Oncescu, J. 22
opportunity costs: and stadium attendance 52, 58, **62**, 64, **67**, 68, 114–15, **117**; and TV ratings 78, **83–4**, 87, 90, 122, **124**
organizational ecology 21–2, 24, 27–8
organizational niches 24, 27–8, 39, 69
out-migration 22–3, 24–5, 26, 27–8, 35, 44, 99

Pan, W. 111, 127
Paniagua, A. 22
patriotism 10–11, 12, 71
Pawlowski, T. 51, 52, 53, 54, 112
pay gap 3–4, 7–9
Pfister, G. 14
Pierson, P. 16, 25
policies: gender policies before and after reunification 7–9; interpretative effects of 16, 17, 25,

26, 27, 98; legacies of 6–9, 16, 17, 25–8, 30, 39, 44, 45, 97–9; policy feedback 16–17; as political forces 16, 25; resource effects of 17, 25, 27
Politbüro des Zentralkomitees 14–15
political systems 4, 7–8
Pommerehne, W. 52, 53, 54
professionalization 48, 50, 70, 74, 100
public service broadcasters (PSBs) 72, 91, 99

quality of soccer, and stadium attendance 47–8, 52–3, 54–5, 55–6, **61**, 64, 65, **66**, 69, 112–13, **117**

rankings of women's national soccer teams *2*, 77–8, 103, **104**
research methodology 18–19
resource competition 27–8, 45
resource effects of policies 17, 25, 27
reunification 6, 8, 9, 16, 20, 26, 27
Rhineland **34**, 35, **37**, **40**, **43**
Roose, H. 97
Rosso, E. 27–8
Rottmann, H. 52, 53, 54
Rowe, D. 91
rural restructuring 22–4, 26, 27–8, 44, 99

Saarland **34**, **38**, 39, **40**, **43**
Saxony-Anhalt 32, **34**
Schleswig-Holstein **34**, **38**, **41**, **43**
schools 23
Schram, S.F. 16
Schröder, B. 27
Schröder, Chancellor Gerhard 72, 90
Scraton, S. 18
Seitz, F. 52, 53, 54
Selmer, N. 10
semi-professional status 48
sexualization of players 73
SG Praunheim **56**
SGs (sport communities) 25–6
Simmons, R. 54, 59, 115
Sloan, L.R. 92
socio-economic status 3, 5–6, 96
Soss, J. 16
South Baden **34**, **38**, 39, **41**, **43**
South West Germany **34**, 35, **38**, 39, **41**, **43**

Index 153

spatial dimension of sport 21–5
sport communities (SGs) 25–6
sport geography 21–2
stadium attendance: analysis of
attendance data 55–9, **56**, *58*;
attendance levels 59–69, *60*, **61**–3,
66–8; data sources and datasets
111–19; determinants of 51–5; and
sporting quality 47–8, 52–3, 54–5,
55–6, **61**, 64, 65, **66**, 69, 112–13,
117; and stadium quality 52, 55,
57, *58*, **61**, 64, **66**, 69, 113–14,
116–17
Stadtmann, G. 51, 52, 53, 54
Stäglin, R. 53
Stahler, K. 3
subcultural approach to leisure 24
suffrage 3
survival of teams: in Frauen-
Bundesliga (FBL) 48, *49*; at
grassroots level 30, 31, **34**, 34, *35*,
39–46, **40–3**, 107–8
Switzerland 2, *2*

team survival *see* survival of teams
television broadcasts *see* TV ratings/
coverage
Thölke, Wim 71–2
Thuringia 32, **34**, 41, **43**
ticket prices 55, 58
Tonts, M. 26
Trappe, H. 7, 8
traveling costs, and stadium
attendance 52, 58, **62**, 64, **67**, 114
TSG 1899 Hoffenheim 50
Turbine Potsdam 21, 27
Turnen movement 10, 11
TV ratings/coverage 76–90, *79–80*,
81–7, *88–9*; age of viewers
80, *80*, **81–7**, *88–9*, 90–1, **123**,
127–9; analyzing the popularity
of women's national team
76–8; audience fragmentation
91–2, 99–100; commercial
broadcasters 72, 91; data
sources and dataset 119–29; and
difficulties facing women's team
71–2; first entire broadcast 13;
free-to-air 71, 78, 122; gender
of viewers *80*, **81–7**, *88–9*, 90–1,

92–3, **123**, **127–9**; men's national
team 71, 72; and policy legacies
92; public service broadcasters
(PSBs) 72, 91, 99; and quality
factors 76, 77–8, 80, **81**, **85**,
89–90, 120–1, **123**, **127–9**; trends
of coverage and ratings 78–90,
79–80, **81–7**, *88–9*

uncertainty of outcome (UOH):
data source 112–13, **117**, 121; and
stadium attendance 48, 53–6, **62**,
66–7, 69; and TV ratings 76, 77, 78,
85, 89–90
Union of European Football
Associations (UEFA) 13, 48, 72, 74
United Nations Educational,
Scientific, and Cultural
Organization (UNESCO) 1–2
urban areas: and grassroots soccer
22–3, 30, 31, 32, 34, **36**, 39, **40**, 45,
107, 111; and stadium attendance
57, **61**, 69, 114

Valenti, M. 17, 18–19, 101
VfL Wolfsburg 50, 56, **56**
voluntary organizations 24, 25, 26

weather conditions: data sources
112, 115, **117–18**, 122, **124–5**;
and stadium attendance 52, 58,
62, 64, **67**, 68; and TV ratings
84, **87**, 90
Weimar Republic 11
West Germany: creation of national
league 47; gender policies 7, 8, 9,
75; grass-roots soccer 13, 20, 26,
34, 35, *35*, **37–8**, 39, **40–1**, 41, **43**,
44, 45, 99; TV ratings *80*, *88–9*;
and reunification 6, 8, 9, 16, 20,
26, 27; women's soccer in (general)
12–14, 98
Whiteside, E. 93
Williams, J. 74, 98
Workers' Gymnastic and Sport
Association (ATSB) 11
World Cups: 1954 men's 12, 71;
1970 women's unofficial 13; 1981
women's unofficial 13; 1999
women's 50; 2003 women's 65,

154 Index

70; 2007 women's 65; 2010 men's 73; 2011 women's 59, 60, 70, 73, 74, 78, 79, 88; 2014 men's 71; 2015 women's 74; 2019 women's 74; data sources/datasets 121, 122, **123**; impact on popularity of women's soccer 73–4, 77–78, 79, **81**, **85**, 88, 90

WSV Wolfsburg-Wendschott **56**

Zwanziger, Theo 14
Zwetkow, Wladimir 21